ProficiencyBench

Providing Value in Your Workplace

Phillip Selleh

CBA Press
6440 Sky Pointe Dr #140-550
Las Vegas, Nevada 89131

Copyright © 2019 by Phillip Selleh.

All rights reserved. No part of this publication may be reproduced, distributed, or transmitted in any form or by any means, including photocopying, recording, or other electronic or mechanical methods, without the prior written permission of the publisher, except in the case of brief quotations embodied in critical reviews and certain other noncommercial uses permitted by copyright law. For permission requests, write to the publisher, addressed "Attention: Permissions Coordinator," at the address below.

CBA Press
6440 Sky Pointe Dr #140-550
Las Vegas, Nevada 89131
www.cbapress.com

ProficiencyBench: Providing Value in Your Workplace / Phillip Selleh. — 1st ed.
ISBN-13: 978-1-7338309-0-4

Dedication

This book is dedicated to the many service members I met at Walter Reed National Military Medical Center who wanted to pursue a career outside of military service. Through their desires, I found the inspiration to write this book and aid in their transitions into the business world. I thank the talented doctors and medical staff at Walter Reed for their compassionate care and motivation. Through their hard work, I discovered the value of self-management, communication, and collaboration in excelling in any professional career. Finally, I acknowledge my family and friends. Through their enduring love and support during my injuries, hospitalizations, and time away from home, I unearthed the passion to continue serving others in my civilian life.

May this book help anyone beginning their journey into a professional career.

Table of Contents

Introduction 1
How to Commit to Success 7
How to Set and Achieve Powerful Goals 21
How to Adjust to Your Workplace Environment 41
How to Make Decisions and Solve Problems 59
How to Embrace the Benefits of Stress Management 81
Conclusion 99

Introduction

If you are like many Americans, your daily work routine might follow a pattern like this:

***

You arrive to work, sit at your desk, and immediately begin working on the reports your supervisor assigned you the day before, not bothering to prioritize your tasks or review your personal agenda. You keep your head down until the reports are complete, passing up the opportunity to visit your boss in his or her office to discuss a project that sounds interesting to you; surely your constant attention to work will speak for itself.

You work diligently until your lunch hour, when you and a few coworkers meet at the local cantina for some Tex-Mex. After lunch, you return to your office and resume your work. You consider altering one of your projects to address a major issue, but you succumb to your worries of failing and instead do nothing; maybe you will solve this problem another day. Progress is slow, but you manage to complete your reports by the end of the day.

Five o'clock approaches and you hastily submit your assignments in an email to your manager. You also ask for directions on your next project, as you are not sure how to solve a problem you encounter. Exhausted from your daily hassles, you quickly grab your jacket and leave the office, making sure to give the office assistant a wave as you dash into the closing elevator doors. Another day is finished.

***

INTRODUCTION

Is there anything wrong with the office routine depicted above? After all, you manage to complete all of your work on time, which speaks to your ability to meet deadlines. You are dependable and reliable, as evidenced by the fact that your boss does not micromanage you throughout the work day. However, if your average work day is like the example above, *you are not making yourself indispensable to your company.*

In today's increasingly competitive marketplace, companies cannot afford to hire employees who adhere to merely a single role. These employees fulfill functional obligations, but do not add any real value to the company that cannot be found elsewhere. These dispensable employees are passed over for new project roles and promotions. They also tend to be professionally surpassed by employees who understand how to make themselves indispensable.

Employment has not always been this way. In fact, as little as twenty years ago, businesses hired a multitude of employees to complete a single task. In the 1990s, America was the sole economic superpower. Employees could afford to charge what they wanted, when they wanted, to whomever they wanted. But with the emergence of new economic titans like China, India, and Brazil, the United States workplace quickly realized that the status quo could not continue. With competitors charging pennies on the dollar for the same work, United States businesses discovered that keeping "one-trick" employees on the taskforce was incredibly expensive. The onslaught of the Great Recession only highlighted this need to eliminate excess costs.

INTRODUCTION

Making yourself indispensable to your company is now critical to achieving both your professional and personal goals. To be considered indispensable in your workplace, you need more than the ability to successfully complete your daily tasks and responsibilities. To better understand how proficiency in the workplace requires more than a basic ability to complete job duties, consider the following example:

***

Example: Joe

Joe is hired as an administrative assistant at a mid-sized company that specializes in selling vintage and indie clothing online. Although the company was founded only a few years ago, it is growing aggressively, and is beginning to cater to an international market. As a result of this growth, employees experience a significant shift in their roles and responsibilities, resulting in many new opportunities for career advancement. Joe is searching for opportunities to provide real value in his company, but he encounters the following difficulties:

- ✗ **Joe rarely demonstrates his admirable personal characteristics.** He keeps to himself and hopes that his work will display his hardworking attitude. Unfortunately, with the increasing demands of the company, Joe's integrity, consistency, and self-discipline go unnoticed by his managers.

- ✗ **Joe does not have a clear understanding of his professional and personal goals.** Although his changing company offers many opportunities for growing his career, he is not sure what job role he seeks or how he might go about achieving this. Joe is also not particularly inspired by his work, which damages his motivation to adopt new responsibilities.

- ✗ **Joe is not settled in his new workplace.** He is not sure who to refer to when he needs assistance, and he has difficulty establishing solid relationships with his coworkers and managers.

- ✗ **Joe is unsure of his ability to make decisions.** This becomes especially problematic when Joe's manager is suddenly called away from the office to attend a family emergency, and Joe is left in a position of great responsibility.

- ✗ **Joe has difficulty coping with the stress of his work.** As his company plans to launch its new website, Joe becomes frantic about meeting absurd deadlines, and his stress places him at risk of burning out.

***

Valuable business skills are not always acquired from industry-specific knowledge or possession of an advanced degree from a prestigious institution. If you want to achieve professional success, attain greater satisfaction in your work, earn more responsibilities, gain the trust of your managers, and become a prized member of your workplace, you will benefit from mastering the following valuable business skills:

- ✔ **Committing to the Character Strengths of Success.** Becoming an indispensable employee is about identifying your inspiration and projecting a persona of confidence, competence, and reliability.

- ✔ **Setting and Achieving Powerful Goals.** Achieving desired results depends on your ability to set powerful and realistic work goals that guide your professional journey.

- ✔ **Adjusting to the Demands of Your Workplace Environment.** In order to demonstrate your value as an employee, you must integrate yourself within your company by developing positive relationships and adhering to standard workplace norms.

- ✔ **Making Dependable Decisions and Solving Workplace Problems.** To be successful in the workplace, you must be capable of making rational decisions while also solving problems that jeopardize your achievements.

✔ **Embracing the Benefits of Stress Management.** Professional success depends on your ability to manage your stress levels in such a way that you do not succumb to the burnout that often afflicts employees in the corporate world.

These skills might seem somewhat basic, especially in comparison to some of the more advanced skills that managers and CEOs might possess. However, the areas listed above are some of the most essential skills, and can be learned through constant diligence and practice. When these valuable business skills have become automatic habits for you, your likelihood of becoming a highly valued employee in any workplace increases dramatically.

Remember, employees who only "keep their heads down" and complete their work rarely become successes in the working world. Instead, the employees who make themselves indispensable are those who become established business leaders. This book is designed to help you learn the processes involved in making yourself indispensable.

INTRODUCTION

Readers should expect to enhance their value in the workplace by learning the business skills that are essential to success. After these critical elements have been examined, we will explore how you can easily overcome some of the most significant obstacles that plague employees. This book contains in-depth lessons on the topics of committing to success, setting and achieving goals, adjusting to your workplace, making decisions and solving problems, and managing stress. Throughout these lessons, you will find helpful examples, tips, techniques, and checklists for practically applying this information to your own professional career. These business skills, if practiced and implemented, will transform you into the ideal indispensable employee that companies desire. Let us begin by discovering the valuable business skills that will aid you in adding value to your workplace from day one.

CHAPTER 1

How to Commit to Success

Before we delve into the business skills of success, let us examine what success means. The concept of success is not an all-inclusive term to be applied at random. Success must be tangible, concrete, and motivational.

There may be as many definitions of success as there are individual human beings. However, success often refers to acquiring the resources a person and his or her loved ones need to be physically, mentally, and emotionally happy. Success also means experiencing the satisfaction of productivity and a job well done. Success often entails experiencing a sense of fulfillment in relation to the world and to others.

Success can only be defined on an individual basis. However, all these definitions of success typically require tenacity, dedication, and motivation to achieve. These are the same skills that are required to make you an indispensable member of your workplace, which in turn may help you achieve any vision of success you might have. Whether you are racing for a new position or simply wanting to earn more responsibilities in your current role, the skills described in this book will help you get there; and thankfully, they are easier to amass than you might think. While the process of personal change is often difficult, practicing the techniques in this book will enhance your skillsets and help you become more valuable to any company you work for.

There are many definitions of success, but none are as important as your own. Consider the following steps to clarify what a successful life means for you:

1. **Envision your ideal successful life.** Find a quiet space in your home, turn off your phone and email, and allow yourself 10 to 20 minutes to let your stress melt away. When you feel relaxed and revitalized, start envisioning your ideal successful life, whether that means spending more time with your family or knowing your workplace contributions are making a positive impact on the world.

2. **Focus on as many specific details as possible.** If you want more time with family, who specifically would you spend more time with? If you want to make a positive impact through your workplace contributions, what specific impact would you make? What will your ideal successful life look, sound, and feel like? How would you know if you were actually achieving your successful life? The more detailed you your visions of success, the more tangible and concrete they will become.

3. **Record your visions of success in a personal notebook or journal.** You may even want to create a success vision board with images of your ideal lifestyle. This will bring your vision of success into reality. When you are specific about what success means to you, you will be more likely to take concrete steps toward achieving your vision.

Consider writing a personal mission statement, a simple declaration of your identity and purpose. Personal mission statements often consist of one or two sentences that clearly define:

- Your personality traits

- Your skills and abilities
- Your values, dreams, and passions
- Your ideal impact on people you encounter

For example, one person's mission statement might read, "To use my charisma, creativity, and passion for learning to inspire positive change in my community." Another person's mission statement might read, "To provide the support and encouragement others need to pursue their dreams." Remember to make a mission statement unique to your own life principles, aspirations, and goals. This process will help you define your own success and proceed through life in accordance with your vision. After creating your own personal mission statement, consider posting it somewhere visible, reviewing it daily, and expressing it to other people in your life.

Success can be a challenging commitment unless you know exactly what you are striving for. That is why it is critical to outline precisely what success means to you before committing to it. It is not enough to say you want to be successful; you need to carefully outline the goals, milestones, and outcomes that will help you arrive at that state. Keep your success journal, vision board, or personal mission statement close to you. Offering yourself daily reminders of what success means will provide the inspiration, motivation, and dedication you need to move forward.

Focus on Your Success

Most aspects of business success reside in the mind. Successful people know the key to staying focused on their visions of success in a busy world is their abilities to visualize their desired outcomes, clear their minds, and avoid distractions. Let us start with three powerful tips that will help you stay focused and primed for success.

Visualize Your Success

Visualizing success, either through your own thoughts or a graphic representation, starts a subconscious process toward achieving it. People sometimes sense or catch one another's ideas and attitudes in an unspoken way. If you are exuding visualizations of your own success, your confidence and assurance will likely catch the attention of company leaders, which may reap benefits for you as a result.

Clear Your Mind

A key aspect of success is starting each day feeling calm and clearheaded. The process of clearing your mind might involve refreshing your memory of tasks to be achieved each day with lists, calendars, or a quick mental summary of your project goals, priorities, and plan components. Some individuals find affirmations, meditation, prayer, or other spiritual activities to contribute towards centering and focusing themselves; these activities allow them to start each day with a "clean slate" and inner refreshment. Inspirational readings help many to organize their minds around beneficial thoughts that melt away extraneous details and focus their mental worlds on what is truly important. Early morning physical exercise is also a wonderful way to clear the mind, start the body's systems, and increase blood flowing to the brain.

Avoid Distractions

Due to an abundance of electronics and lightning-fast communication, we nowadays live in a distracting world. Businesses have noticed how much time their employees spend surfing the internet rather than doing their jobs, even as they appear to be diligently absorbed in their screens. Electronic devices absorb minutes and even hours of our time. How much of your day is lost to idle conversations? We are more productive when we use our time efficiently and are focused exclusively on accomplishing necessary tasks. This focused work time makes free time feel even sweeter.

While we have suggested that a balanced life leads to happiness, we should not lose focus on our goals. Review your written goals and personal mission statements to refresh your memories, remember what you want to achieve, and allow your priorities settle accordingly. Measure your activities based on whether they are bringing you closer to your goals or leading you farther away from them. By judging your activities, you can assess whether or not you are focused on your vision of success.

Visualizing success, mentally clearing your mind, and avoiding distractions are mental components of success. Some may consider these to be the most important components of success, as success depends heavily upon what you project internally. Let us continue to pursue your vision by exploring the character strengths of success.

Commit to the Traits of Success

To lead a successful life, you need a foundation of character strengths inherent to success. Certain traits lead to the kind of long term success you have just envisioned, where multiple satisfactions add up to a prosperous and fulfilling life.

Now that you have outlined exactly what success means to you, let us explore how you can commit your mind and emotions to your specific vision by embracing the traits of professional success. Traits including integrity, character, persistence, consistency, and other vital characteristics will help you become more valuable to your company.

Fortunately, these traits are not scarcely bestowed upon only a lucky few. They can all be learned and mastered with practice. Though the process of learning these traits might be difficult, remember that they *are learnable*. Let this be a motivating factor for you as you work through the material in this book. Like a muscle, a character trait can be strengthened and improved upon until you achieve your optimal results. For example, even if you do not consider yourself the funniest person on the block, you can still develop a sense of humor, which might help you avoid taking disappointments too seriously or letting angry clients ruin your positive mood.

Let us explore some of the traits that will help in your quest for business success. As we cover each trait, you will find a list of techniques you can use to embrace and strengthen your execution of that characteristic during your daily activities.

Demonstrate Integrity

Integrity, or the act of honoring your word, means as soon as you realize you cannot deliver on your promises, you take ownership of any mistake and minimize the inconvenience to those affected. Commitment to one's self is as important to integrity as one's commitment to others. If you promise yourself that you will wake up at 6:00 a.m. each day to perform one hour of exercise, but then proceed to break that commitment, the habit of breaking promises becomes a standard part of your life. As a result, other people will inevitably perceive you as unreliable and undependable. To maintain your integrity, use the following techniques:

☐ **Reward yourself for completing difficult tasks and activities as promised.** For example, suppose you promise your boss you will complete a project within two business days. After you have fulfilled this commitment, reward yourself with a small treat or item that you have been interested in. The act of rewarding your efforts will go a long way towards making integrity habitual.

Task:	Reward:
Print login instructions for interns	Eat a snack bar
Propose new policy to supervisor	See a movie later

☐ **Practice honesty in all your communication with bosses, peers, and family members.** By being honest in all your dealings, others will never wonder if you have an ulterior motive. Honesty is critical to displaying integrity, and you should practice it in all facets of your life.

☐ **Surround yourself with dependable and reliable people.** Maintaining your integrity will be much easier if you keep ideal company. If you have friends and family members who consistently keep their promises while displaying honesty and compassion in their dealings, you will more easily understand their behaviors and practice them in your own life.

Demonstrate Character

Character is far more than one's personality. One's character encompasses the virtues or strengths that are developed through life, often with the assistance and instruction of parents, teachers, and mentors. You can become a person of favorable character by learning about your ideal virtues and acting accordingly. When you act with virtue, you will generate trust in those around you. Enhance your character by employing the following techniques:

☐ **Be fair and diplomatic whenever possible.** Displaying good character means ensuring that everyone is treated fairly and with the respect they deserve. For example, being kind and polite to waiters reflects favorably on your character, while being rude often indicates your inability to empathize with others.

- [ ] **Always keep your promises.** In the event that keeping a promise is impossible, do not report your failing at the last minute. For example, suppose you promise your uncle that you will drive him to the hospital for a doctor's appointment. Do *not* call him the morning of the appointment to inform him that you cannot fulfill your promise. Instead, adjust your schedule to remain true to your commitment. If, due to emergency circumstances, you absolutely cannot drive him to the hospital, call a cab for your uncle to ensure he is treated fairly.

Demonstrate Persistence

Persistence involves standing firm even in the face of discouragement and seemingly insurmountable obstacles. Those able to persist through difficult situations are better equipped to overcome hurdles and achieve success. You must persist while you are at work in spite of the temptation to take shortcuts. This will increase your likelihood of actually achieving your goals. If you want to embrace persistence in your own quest for business success, consider repeating the following mantra to yourself every day before arriving to work:

- ✔ "I will persevere until I succeed. Every time I move forward, I am succeeding. I will never consider defeat and I will continue to move forward even in the face of hardships. I will never let words like 'quit' and 'impossible' enter my vocabulary—instead, I will use words like 'can' and 'will.' If I am not successful at first, I will always try again."

You might also create your own mantra if you find this one to be unsuitable. A potent mantra will help you embrace the power of persistence in your own life.

Demonstrate Consistency

A consistent person will repeatedly conduct tasks in the same manner. However, realize that consistency does not always have a positive correlation. For example, someone might be consistently terrible at performing a certain task. Instead, one should aspire for positive consistency in the following areas:

- Clarifying project needs
- Producing high-quality work
- Completing tasks on time
- Keeping commitments

The type of consistency with a positive correlation involves repeatedly performing tasks well by applying yourself and fulfilling your promise to produce the best work possible. Practice consistency by utilizing the following techniques:

☐ **Perform every task to high-quality standards.** Maintaining the same standards requires you to find the passion to conduct your work professionally, even when you are assigned to relatively mundane tasks. For example, if you are asked to enter data into a spreadsheet, consider how the company will make use of your spreadsheet. It may be a crucial point of discussion during a meeting, or it may help your manager make a critical business decision. Identifying how your work is important to others will hugely benefit your ability to keep the quality of your work consistent.

CHAPTER 1: Commit to Success

☐ **Always keep your promises**. This is a consistent behavior that will teach those around you to always rely on your word.

☐ **If you have trouble upholding consistency in your work, take a break.** Not everyone has the ability to maintain high levels of passion and quality all day, every day of the week. In fact, people often succumb to mental burnout when they try to. If you realize you are losing focus from exhaustion or are generally not producing your best work, walk around the office or, if appropriate, give yourself a few hours off to rest your brain. The most valued employees understand that their health and wellness is equally as important as submitting work on time.

Demonstrate Hard Work

Hard work is a crucial component of becoming a valuable member of your workplace. When you understand how your contributions to your company are vital to its success, you will put your best work into what you do, regardless of whether or not you will be rewarded. To encourage your habit of working hard, use the following techniques:

☐ **Forego the need for praise**. While recognition for each and every one of your tasks is certainly reassuring—especially if this comes from a supervisor—do not allow praise to be the only motivation for your productivity and dedication. Hard work should stem from an internal desire to always do your best. Complete each task to the best of your ability, not for the sake of receiving commendations from a manager, but for how it reflects on you as an employee and a person.

☐ **Be aware of the time you spend on distracting activities.** Spending too much time online checking your email or browsing the internet significantly reduces your productivity. Be mindful of the distractors that exist within your workplace. Keep a time log or use a stopwatch to track the time you spend distracted from work. Eliminate or minimize your distractions to ensure that you are always working hard.

Demonstrate Self-Discipline

Despite the term's negative connotations, self-discipline presses you to generate high-quality work which helps you achieve your personal successes. Self-discipline is an incredibly valuable skill to possess, as it provides you with the drive and determination to work hard without a manager or supervisor micromanaging when and how submit your work. Self-discipline enables you to complete tasks, not necessarily because you want to, but because you are striving toward a loftier goal. To encourage the development of self-discipline in your life, implement the following techniques:

- ☐ **Connect your work to a greater goal.** For example, if you are tasked with a particularly uninteresting budget spreadsheet for your manager, consider that spreadsheet as a tool which will communicate your dedication to the company and capacity for hard work. If you view mundane tasks as crucial steps toward a larger goal, you will find the discipline you need for carrying on with your work.

- ☐ **Set smaller personal goals.** For example, if you want to lose twenty pounds, create a workout schedule over the course of the next month with the goal of losing 1 pound per week, then follow your plan. When you prove to yourself that you are capable of achieving smaller goals on your own, apply your newfound self-discipline to bigger goals in both your professional and personal lives.

Demonstrate Passion

When a task fills you with a strong sense of passion or purpose, you are more likely to dedicate yourself to the hard work necessary for completing it. Passion is what pushes you to continue "marching forward" toward your goal when you are tired, frustrated, or overwhelmed. Projecting passion also helps other people in your company recognize your dedication to your job and its responsibilities. When your managers see you are truly dedicated to your work, they may provide you with additional responsibilities or training opportunities. Unfortunately, passion does not always come easily, especially if you lack a genuine desire to complete your work. In such cases, implement the following techniques to unlock your passion:

☐ **Learn more about your industry.** Learn what your industry does for the world, and what role you play in it. Understanding how your work factors into the greater good of your company, your industry, or even the world will infuse passion into otherwise banal procedures.

> Input sales into spreadsheet
> ↳ My company will know if it has enough product (medical supplies) in stock
>   ↳ My company will order new product if needed
>   ↳ My company will distribute its products to hospitals
>   ↳ Hospitals will save people's lives

- [ ] **Stay late at work.** While you do not need to keep yourself at the office hours after closing, staying an additional 15 minutes or half hour demonstrates your commitment to completing your work. Occasionally staying late also helps you avoid garnering a harmful reputation for sprinting out the door as soon as the work day ends.

- [ ] **Connect with passionate employees.** Passion is incredibly contagious, so spend some time talking to people who love their jobs. Their attitudes might inspire you to find purpose in your own job, or even seek out a job you are truly passionate about.

Demonstrate a Sense of Humor

You do not need the kind of humor displayed by standup comedians. Rather, you should strive to develop the humor used to accept the things you cannot change, as well as to avoid taking yourself too seriously. Setbacks, disappointments, and disagreements will eventually materialize in the workplace, and a sense of humor will help keep these disappointments in perspective. This prevents you from internalizing your setbacks and using them as an excuse for failing to move forward with your goals. Get your "funny bone" working with the following techniques:

- [ ] **Keep fun activities in your life.** Participating in fun activities is especially important if you find your work stressful or frustrating. Go for a run, spend time with friends, or take a weekend trip with the family. These healthy and joyful activities will put work setbacks into perspective and remind you that they do not constitute your entire life.

- [ ] **If you experience a setback or disappointment, talk to a friend or family member.** Having such an outlet is a great way to avoid taking setbacks too seriously, as your listener might help you keep a realistic perspective and realize that some disappointments are not nearly as severe as they first seem.

This chapter offers you a better understanding of your vision of success and the traits that will make you an indispensable component of your workplace. Business skills do not need to be complicated. In fact, some of the most powerful business skills are also crucial to living happy and healthy personal lives. By using the techniques described in this chapter, you will lay the groundwork for establishing yourself in your company, which will bring you closer to your career goals.

In the next chapter, we will discuss how you might use these skills to achieve goals and realize success.

CHAPTER 2

How to Set and Achieve Powerful Goals

If your journey to career success is like a road trip, then your goals are like the labels on a map that guide you to make turns, take exits, and ultimately arrive at your destination. You cannot get there unless you know where you are going. Without clearly defined and outlined goals, you will find it difficult to determine whether you are progressing toward success or going completely off course.

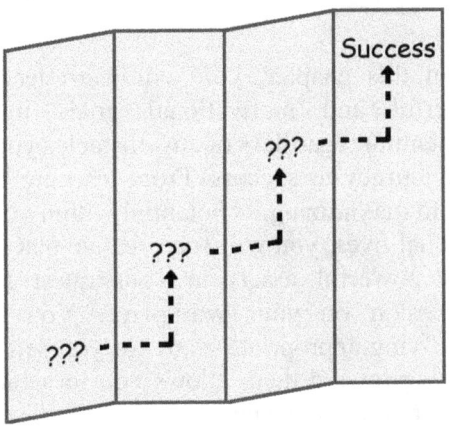

In order to achieve the success you defined in the previous chapter, you will need more than your vision and the character strengths associated with professional success. You must first understand how goals place you on your ideal path for the future. Whether your dreams involve helping your community or simply becoming more valuable in your organization, goals provide you with specific steps to achieve what you desire. Goals are more than simple milestones that might be achieved through hard work and effort. In fact, goals are vital to keeping you moving in the right direction, maintaining your progress, and alerting you when you have gone off track.

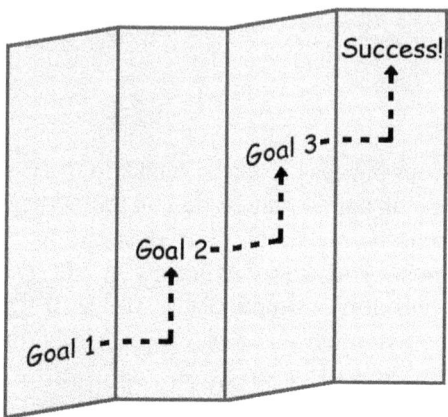

In this chapter, you will learn techniques for setting powerful and motivational goals that maintain your momentum regardless of any obstacles you may encounter on your journey to success. From learning how to define your goal to maximizing its potential within your professional and personal lives, you will soon realize that a goal is one of the most powerful assets in your quest to make a lasting impression on your workplace. You will discover that identifying appropriate goals for yourself and systematically working toward them allows you to achieve more than you have previously thought possible.

Define Your Goals

Defining your goals plays a critical role in your ability to achieve your professional dreams. It is not enough to create broad overviews of what you want to achieve such as, "I want to be more productive." Defining a powerful goal entails understanding where you currently stand in relation to your objective, what you need to do to move toward your objective, and how you can measure your progress along the way.

Clarify Your Goal

Goals are simply dreams with deadlines. However, unlike dreams, which may be vague and overly ambiguous, goals should have specific outcomes. A goal is not completed simply by doing your best. You are far more likely to accomplish goals that have clarity. For example, instead of nebulously stating a goal, "I want to be more productive," you might specify the outcome being pursued. You might revise this goal to, "I want to meet more of the deadlines imposed by my supervisor," or, "I want to ensure more of my customers report satisfaction." Clarify your goal by answering the following questions:

- What specifically am I trying to gain?
- Who or what is involved in this goal?
- If I mention "more" or "less," how much or how many?
- What am I comparing this to?

Make Your Goal Measurable

A powerful goal is one that can be objectively measured, ideally with tangible evidence. If you do not have a method for measuring your goal, how will you know when you have achieved it? Define your goals in numbers if possible, as this makes your progress quantifiable, and makes tracking your goals an enjoyable and motivating activity. For example, the vague statement, "I want to meet more of the deadlines imposed by my supervisor," could be specified even further and thereby made measurable. You might revise this goal to, "I will meet a minimum of 95 percent of the deadlines imposed by my supervisor." Using quantifiable criteria to measure your goals will make you better equipped to track your progress, adjust your actions as needed, and know when you have achieved your desired results.

Make Your Goal Time Sensitive

Goals have more power when you understand the deadlines attached to them. Some goals are impossible to achieve if they seem as though they will never end. Remedy this feeling by giving your largest goal a final deadline, as this gives you a specific end date to push toward. For example, the specific and measurable goal above, "I will meet a minimum of 95 percent of the deadlines imposed by my supervisor" could be modified with the addition of a particular timeline. You might revise this goal to, "By March 31st, I will meet a minimum of 95 percent of the monthly deadlines imposed by my supervisor." Setting this deadline empowers you to take action to ensure you match your goal's schedule. This due date also prevents you from procrastinating for years before finally improving your work performance. By setting a final deadline, if you begin to lose your motivation or determination, you can think of that specific date and realize all your hard work might eventually pay off.

✖
> "I want to be more productive."

✔
> "By March 31st, I will meet a minimum of 95 percent of the monthly deadlines imposed by my supervisor."

Repeat this process for each of the goals that lead to your vision of success. Formulate a detailed list of what you need to accomplish. Some goals will have subgoals grouped within them, and all goals will have action steps that lead to their accomplishments. The above steps are vital starting points when setting powerful goals within your professional life. In the next section you will learn tips and techniques for maximizing accomplishment of your goals and harvesting your desired results faster.

Set Action Plans for Your Goals

Setting goals plays a crucial role in your accomplishment of specific successes, but there is a difference between simply pointing at someone's job-related credentials and saying, "I want that," and taking concrete steps towards earning those same credentials for yourself in the future. Unless you also create action steps dedicated to a goal's accomplishment, setting a goal will hardly be effective.

Clarifying specific goals helps you generate action steps to achieve desirable results. Recall the exercise you performed in Chapter 1, when you envisioned what success means to you. Focusing on the smallest details probably made success seem more tangible. The details may have provided you with a clear understanding of what you needed to do to achieve it. Goals follow the same rule. Through being as specific as possible with your goals, you will uncover tangible steps towards their completion. Review the following examples of an ambiguous goal and a specific goal, then consider the substantial differences between the two:

***

✗ Example #1: Ambiguous Goal

Jessica wants to attend a prestigious training program held at the end of the year. When Jessica tells her manager about the training program, her manager seems unsure of the value the program would provide. Jessica sets a goal to follow up with her manager about the training program a few weeks before registration closes. When she does, her manager's opinion has not changed, and he refuses to give Jessica the permission she needs to attend the program.

CHAPTER 2: Set and Achieve Powerful Goals

***

✓ Example #2: Specific Goal with Action Steps

Jessica wants to attend a prestigious training program held at the end of the year. After her manager indicates his uncertainty regarding the training program's benefits, Jessica sets a goal to convince her manager that the training program will provide excellent value. She creates an in-depth presentation that outlines exactly how the program will benefit her role, then presents it to her manager months before registration closes. She also devotes longer hours to her work, hoping to impress her manager with her hard work and motivation. Furthermore, Jessica connects with previous program attendees via LinkedIn and gathers their feedback regarding the value of the program. Jessica's manager is convinced by her hard work and research; he decides to give her permission to sign up for the training program.

***

The differences between these two examples are profound. In both examples Jessica set the goal of attending the prestigious training program. However, the similarities end there. In the first example, Jessica made no effort to convince her manager to allow her to attend the training program beyond simply asking again at a later time. In the second example, however, she took concrete action steps towards achieving her goal: by working hard and taking time to properly convey the benefits of this program, she addressed potential concerns or issues that might have otherwise arisen.

Setting specific goals involves much more than simply identifying something you want. It involves creating a timeline of actions that will increase your probability of achieving your goal. These action steps create momentum toward your goal, which increases your likelihood of arriving at it. To set action steps toward your own goals, utilize the following steps:

1. **Work backwards from your identified goal.** For example, suppose you set a goal of advancing your skillset by earning a job-related professional certificate. Instead of focusing on what next steps to take, pretend you already have that certificate and you are reflecting on the steps you took to get there. You might imagine that you participated in online classes, which you discovered after asking your supervisor for suggestions about what skills you might improve. Working backwards will help you gain a more realistic idea of what steps you need to take to achieve a goal.

2. **List steps toward your goal.** When considering a goal, break it into manageable, assignable tasks. Look at what steps logically need to be completed first in order to move forward within your goal's timeline. Use the ideas you generated in the previous step as a reference. Be as concrete and specific as possible; precision is key. For example, keeping with the goal to earn a professional certificate, your list of action steps might include identifying relevant and potentially valuable certificates, determining your eligibility, registering for classes, participating in classes, preparing for the final exam, and finally passing the final exam.

3. **Give each action step a deadline.** For example, if you are preparing to take a final exam as part of a professional certificate program, you might set specific and timely action steps for studying three subtopics each afternoon for one week. This timeline gives you markers with which you can compare your progress. At the end of each day you can count the number of subtopics you studied to determine if you are proceeding according to your schedule. If you miss a deadline, you might increase the number of subtopics you study the next afternoon, or you might adjust the action item to be more realistic. Either way, setting deadlines for your action steps helps you

determine whether you are achieving your goal as originally anticipated.

> **Earn a professional certificate (Action Steps):**
> Ask supervisor what skills to improve - due 8/16
> Identify relevant/valuable certifications - due 8/23
> Search for available certificate programs - due 8/26
> Determine my eligibility - due 8/30
> Enroll in program - due 9/2
> Prepare for final exam - due 9/18
> Pass final exam - due 9/20

Pursue Your Goals

When you have set your goals and created action steps to achieve them, take the following steps to pursue your goals and ensure your efforts return rewards.

Connect Your Goals to Meaningful Benefits

Connecting your professional goals to personal benefits will preserve your motivation even when you feel exhausted by your hard work. For example, if you plan to earn a certain job position, and you have logged numerous hours of hard work to convince your managers to give you this responsibility, you might understandably feel exhausted. However, if you focus on how the change in duties will benefit you or your family (more opportunities to display your interests, less stress to "bring home," etc.), you will more easily surmount any discouragement and continue pursuing your goals.

Goals must have personal relevance in your life, even if they are strictly professional. Attaining a new job position certainly has an emotional significance attached to it. For example, a specific job duty or obligation might mean challenging yourself or fulfilling your sense of purpose in life.

Other details associated with a new position, such as financial or hourly allowances, might mean a greater quality of life for your family members.

Adopt a Can-Do Attitude

Your success in the business world begins in your mind. Having a can-do mindset may make all the difference in achieving your goals. When you focus on your future successes, work to achieve your goals, and have an attitude of realistic self-confidence in your abilities, your likelihood of success increases dramatically. If, on the other hand, you do not believe you will achieve what you are working towards, you will lack the motivation necessary for reaching your goals, and you will ultimately fall short of success as a result.

A can-do attitude does not include taking on more than you are able to handle. Keep your goals attainable and your expectations realistic. Unless you are certain that you can accomplish a given task, it is probably better not to accept it in the first place. A can-do attitude does mean, however, that you will not give up on a task before you start, and that you will be willing to challenge any barriers to accomplishment, including those you create for yourself.

Establish a Sense of Ownership

If you want your goal to be successful, you must establish a sense of ownership by holding yourself responsible for the success or failure of your goal. Do not place blame on any person or event for creating obstacles which slow your progress toward business success. Instead, hold yourself accountable for the efforts *you* make to overcome challenges as you climb toward your ultimate dream. Instill a sense of ownership by taking these steps:

- [ ] Restate your goal in terms of how you will work to achieve it.
- [ ] Outline the tasks and responsibilities involved in achieving the goal.
- [ ] Schedule regular brainstorming dates to determine how to continue to be successful.
- [ ] Rearticulate how you will measure the accomplishment of your goal.
- [ ] Celebrate every milestone or deadline you achieve.

By establishing a sense of ownership, you will have the pleasure of taking credit for all your hard work and success when you finally achieve your dream goal.

Enlist an Accountability Partner

The desire to follow through on social expectations is a fantastic motivator. Take advantage of this force by recruiting an accountability partner, a person whom you regularly report to regarding your goals. Accountability partners typically work toward separate goals while providing each other with mutual support. Having an accountability partner offers the following benefits:

- ✔ **An accountability partner holds you responsible for the results you achieve.** This added responsibility may make you more serious about your commitments.

- ✔ **An accountability partner pushes you outside your comfort zone.** Embracing uncomfortable situations might make the difference between success and failure.

- ✓ **An accountability partner provides support and encouragement.** You may find it easier to stay motivated when you have a supporter cheering, "You can do it!"

- ✓ **An accountability partner provides an outside perspective.** A steady source of constructive criticism may be highly useful when assessing progress on goals.

When seeking an accountability partner, first look within your existing social circle. Discussing personal goals will be easier with a spouse, friend, coworker, or person whom you already have regular contact with. If you cannot find an accountability partner among individuals you already interact with, make a post about your search on social media or a message board related to your goal. Individuals with similar goals will be able to offer advice and insight specifically relevant to your own goals. When searching, understand that a reliable accountability partner will have many of the following traits:

- ☐ **This person is available enough for your goal-related needs.** This person should be able to meet with you regularly to discuss your goals.

- ☐ **This person is goal-oriented, industrious, and familiar with setting and achieving goals.** Conversations about goals will be more valuable if the other party understands the basics of successfully pursuing goals.

- ☐ **This person genuinely wants you to succeed.** In addition to being available enough to meet with you, this person should also be emotionally capable of extending interest in your progress.

- ☐ **This person will challenge you to reach your goals.** In order to fulfill the role of accountability partner, this person must hold you accountable for your progress. A person who accepts innumerable excuses will offer little help.

☐ **This person will evoke a sense of accomplishment in you.** When you finally achieve your goals, this person should help you feel victorious, triumphant, and motivated to continue achieving.

After successfully locating a reliable accountability partner, publicly pledge your goal to him or her. Consider writing an informal "commitment contract" which describes any consequences for not achieving your goal. Schedule regular appointments for your accountability partner to listen to your goals, check in on your progress, celebrate any achievements, and explore the reasons for any shortcomings. If you and your accountability partner decide to provide each other with mutual support, remember to engage in his or her goals to the same degree that you want him or her to be engaged in your own. Appointments that take place in person are best, though meeting via Skype, phone, or email is still beneficial. If appropriate, involve your accountability partner in the other goal-setting and goal-achieving techniques described in this chapter as well.

Use Support as Needed

You cannot always be successful alone. Understanding your strengths and weaknesses is important. When you need help, do not hesitate to look to others. Friends and family members can provide the supportive network you need, especially if you are serving long hours at work and need the mental and emotional benefits that come from healthy interpersonal relationships.

Routinely Monitor Your Progress

Setting action steps does not necessarily guarantee success in reaching your goals. Unexpected incidents and setbacks can easily bring your momentum to a halt. To counteract these potential setbacks, make a habit of routinely checking your progress by utilizing the following techniques:

☐ **Be flexible with deadlines and action steps.** Part of maintaining your progress involves determining whether you have set an unrealistic goal or deadline. If, despite working hard, you miss several action item deadlines, consider revising your strategy to be more realistic and attainable. Goals that are too difficult to achieve are often abandoned, so it is in your best interest to make your goals reasonable.

☐ **If you have trouble achieving your goals, ask a friend or family member for feedback.** For example, if you set a goal of earning a promotion only six months after starting at a new company, you might require an outside opinion to realize this is not a realistic expectation. Select a friend or family member who will be honest with you, as this straightforward feedback will shape your realistic and attainable new goals.

Embrace Challenges and Roadblocks

Regardless of how many action items and strategies you use when setting your goals, things rarely go exactly according to plan. However, you should understand that setbacks will not derail the achievement process entirely; rather, they will present interesting challenges that test your ability to surmount them. In fact, the process of overcoming challenges on your way to achieving your ultimate goal makes for a rich and vital learning experience.

Overcome Obstacles

Anything worth striving for will come with some challenges. This is the simple reality of moving forward. Your success will be largely predicated on how you handle the obstacles you encounter. If challenges threaten to derail your goal, take a systematic approach to resolving them. First, identify your obstacles by asking yourself the following questions for each:

- What is the obstacle?
- What are my risks if it persists?
- What will it take to overcome it?
- Can it be easily removed?
- Who will I need to enlist to assist me with resolving it?
- Will it derail my goal if left unattended?
- Will it cost more and how do I fund this cost?

Now that you have all the facts about your obstacle, proceed to determine your revised action plan by asking yourself the following questions:

- What have I decided to do?
- What steps will I take to get through the issue?
- Who will own it?
- When will it be completed?
- What might I continue to do as I work through this challenge?

Now that you have solidified your new action plan, use the following steps to communicate your plan to others and implement the change:

- [ ] Discuss the obstacle with friends or family members and consider any helpful advice they might have.
- [ ] Set expectations for yourself.
- [ ] Proceed with your new action and monitor progress.

There will often be other tasks you should continue to work on while you deal with the obstacle. Consider your overall goal and continue to make progress on any items which are currently attainable.

Record Your Mistakes

Not all goals will go according to plan. In instances where your plans go awry, write down your mistakes so you do not make them again. Consider making a goal journal where you can record your daily efforts towards pursuing your professional goals. If you make an error along your journey to success, record the reasons why that mistake occurred. For example, if you fail to meet your goal of assembling a professional portfolio by the end of the month, consider the reasons for your shortcoming, then record them to make improvements in the future. Perhaps you did not spend enough time revisiting your past projects, or maybe you neglected to ask your friends and family members for needed feedback. Be as specific as possible, as this will help you avoid making similar mistakes in the future.

Forgive yourself for making mistakes. Providing value in the workplace through achieving a goal is *not* an easy task. There may be some setbacks and disappointments, but if you forgive yourself, these misfortunes will not prevent you from attempting to achieve additional goals in the future.

Review Your Results

After you identify your goals and fulfill your action steps, you will inevitably encounter some outcome. Whether this outcome is your desired objective or otherwise, reviewing your results will enable you to improve your goal-setting abilities in the future.

Reward Yourself for Achievements

Rewarding yourself for achievements is especially important when pursuing long-term goals, as even the most passionate and dedicated person might lose motivation otherwise. If you need a boost of positivity to remind yourself of the hard work you have been performing, reward yourself for achieving a specific action item. For example, if you set a goal of embracing a managerial role, and your boss accepts your request to be the acting team leader on an important project team, reward yourself by seeing a movie or buying something you have wanted for some time. These little rewards will keep your motivation up, even when you are in the middle of a long-term goal.

Assess Your Achieved Goals

After the "dust has settled" and your reach the end of the goal achieving process, assess whether or not you were successful. Accomplishing the goal takes you roughly three quarters of the way; the remainder of your journey involves assessing the impact of your accomplishment and determining the steps that will direct you toward your next goal.

When assessing your goal achievement, refer to the plan you made when you initially set the goal. Returning to your original plan is the easiest way to assess your goals, as you reuse the criteria you already formulated for measuring your success. Assemble a comprehensive review of the following goal items:

- What was the goal?
- What action steps did I take?
- What outcome did I expect?
- What results did I achieve?

Next, assess your achievement by asking yourself the following questions:

- Did I meet the criteria I put into place?
  - If so, how did I do it?
  - If not, why do I consider the goal accomplished?
- Do my current results make the goal more attractive or less?
- Do I need to formulate additional goals or extend this one to address some of the results?

When you review your performance, ask yourself the following questions:

- How did I perform?
- How will I use my resources better next time?
- Did I stay focused?
- What were the biggest challenges?
- What accomplishments am I most proud of from the process?
- What do I feel could have used improvement?
- What changes will I make to my next goal implementation?
- What will I continue to do whenever I set a goal?
- What will I change if faced with the same goal in the future?

Even if you did not reap the rewards you expected upon accomplishing your goal, there is a silver lining: everything you learned in the process. Keep your reflections from this debriefing as a point of reference which you can use whenever you set goals in the future. We should learn from both our successes and our failures, so take the time to go through this process.

Reset your goals as you achieve each one. The last thing you want is to remain stagnant, so stretch yourself each time you accomplish a goal. Set each next goal a bit higher than the previous and keep challenging yourself in order to promote personal growth and professional success.

The practice of goal setting may initially seem like a trivial component of ensuring your success, but setting effective goals is a vital part of progressing. If you fail to dedicate time and attention to setting effective goals, you undermine your own journey toward business success.

Goals are more than simple strategies for determining your options; instead, goals are key components and your most valuable assets in pursuing any vision of career success you may have, such as earning a desired job position or finally completing a special project.

CHAPTER 2: Set and Achieve Powerful Goals

In the next chapter, we will explore how to integrate yourself into your workplace.

CHAPTER 3

How to Adjust to Your Workplace Environment

At first glance, adjusting to your workplace environment might seem like one of the less challenging steps in the process of becoming a proficient employee. For example, if you are a veteran looking to apply your skills to a civilian workplace, the process might initially appear trivial when compared to the transition from civilian to military lifestyle. Certainly, the military lifestyle required you to learn how to establish relationships with your peers and meet demands in a timely manner, skills which should undoubtedly be utilized within a business environment.

However, many employees have difficulty adjusting themselves to better fit within their workplace environments, especially when transitioning into a new workplace which is entirely different from those of their previous work experiences. To better understand the challenges of establishing your proficiency within an unfamiliar workplace, consider the following example:

***

Example: Amber
Amber has worked within a university's fundraising and development department for several years, and has recently transitioned to a Fortune 500 environment. In her previous job, she was responsible for interfacing with donors and eliciting donations between $1,000 and $20,000 in value. At her corporate workplace, Amber's position involves managing stakeholders while establishing meetings between

CHAPTER 3: Adjust to Your Workplace Environment

her organization's members and other Fortune 500 leaders. She is also responsible for arranging press releases regarding any major fundraising events that the company holds.

In her first few weeks on the job, Amber is assigned the task of creating a press release for a 5k being held by a local university. She is also charged with ensuring that stakeholders attend the event and are given excellent treatment. Consider some of the following common workplace challenges Amber encounters:

× **Amber is unsure how to handle potentially inappropriate behaviors.** Amber is included in several emails from coworkers which include links to celebrity gossip blogs and entertainment news sites. Some of these links contain stills and videos of inappropriate celebrity tapes, which make Amber extremely uncomfortable. However, her coworkers do not seem bothered by these links. In fact, they often comment on the links with jokes. Amber is unsure of what to do; at her previous workplace she would have reported these inappropriate links immediately, but her current company environment seems to accept these links openly.

× **Amber struggles to keep up with her increased workload.** While Amber was responsible for dealing with donors at her previous nonprofit, her new corporate responsibilities involve arranging the schedules of extremely busy stakeholders. She finds that her time management skills are not as strong as they need to be, and she is struggling to learn quickly.

× **Amber has trouble adapting to the fast-paced culture of her new corporate environment.** At her previous jobs, deadlines were more flexible; in her current job, deadlines arrive rapidly and seem insurmountable. Amber finds it necessary to work a few extra hours several days each week, which is accepted and almost expected of employees at her new workplace.

CHAPTER 3: Adjust to Your Workplace Environment

***

The example above depicts a realistic experience that many new employees encounter on a daily basis. Skills and techniques that might work in one workplace environment might not necessarily work within another. Readers must understand how to successfully adapt to their workplace environments by developing new proficiency skills, all while encouraging the growth of existing abilities. Although this growth process can be challenging, everyone can learn these techniques with diligent practice and persistence.

Now that we have explored some of the challenges inherent to adjusting to a new workplace, let us examine the techniques readers can use to surmount these challenges while growing into proficient and valuable employees.

Assess Your Workplace Environment

Many employees make the common mistake of failing to assess their workplace environments. When transitioning to a new or different workplace, employees must spend some time learning the workplace itself. Unless you know the culture, attitude, and behaviors of a workplace, you will have difficulty uncovering the ideal way of establishing yourself as a valuable employee.

Implement the following techniques, ideally during the first few days or weeks at a new job, to gain a better understanding of the general attitudes of your workplace.

Read Your Organization's Mission Statement

Nearly every organization has a mission statement which articulates its purpose, explains its focus, and answers the question, "Why are we here?" This short statement will transcend simple products and services to outline, on a grander scale, what the company stands for.

CHAPTER 3: Adjust to Your Workplace Environment

Your organization's mission statement might explain some of the values, beliefs, principles, desires, and cultural expectations the organization has for its employees. This mission statement might clarify the importance of your training, the relevance of your skills, and the necessity of your role in the organization's operation. This statement might also clarify your organization's primary goals. This clarity might then offer employees context to their own job roles, thus allowing them to align with the goals of other employees and departments. Furthermore, your organization's mission statement might summarize your organization's strategy. Understanding the business's basic strategy might enable new employees to rapidly discern priorities and decision-making methods. Finally, in addition to understanding what your new workplace expects from you, the mission statement might uncover what you can expect from your workplace. Your organization's mission statement might communicate how employment will benefit you, and how the organization will treat you.

When reading your organization's mission statement, pay attention to the specific words used. Individual words or phrases that "stand out" to you were probably carefully selected for their carried meanings. Allow yourself to be inspired by these words and phrases, as this will ensure that you understand your company's purpose and ways of achieving it. Although understanding your organization's mission statement will be highly useful, adjusting to your workplace environment will happen most naturally when you simply "live" the mission statement through your actions, behaviors, and language. Personally commit to engaging in your organization's stated goals, then go "above and beyond" to help achieve them. Use your organization's mission statement as a reason to persevere whenever you experience low motivation or difficulties with adjusting to your workplace.

CHAPTER 3: Adjust to Your Workplace Environment

Learn from Your Coworkers

One of the most valuable assets you can utilize during your investigative research is the knowledge of an experienced coworker. When you arrive at a new workplace, there is a short span of time during which your new coworkers will offer you vital basic information. You can acquire a great deal of critical knowledge about your new workplace during this "introductory period." Use the following tips to uncover the information you need for successfully adjusting to your work environment:

☐ **Take a coworker out for lunch.** Alternatively, join a small group of employees during their next coffee run. These social environments offer you opportunities to have personal and honest conversations. Your offering a small treat can be significant when convincing people to have truthful discussions with you, especially when you have not yet established a genuine relationship. When you give a fellow employee a small treat or meaningful gesture, he or she will feel obligated to return your favor—psychologists refer to this social norm as the "rule of reciprocity."[1] For example, purchasing a cup of coffee for a coworker could result in you receiving vital information about how to get a one-on-one meeting with a manager.

☐ **Ask your coworkers plenty of questions.** This is one of the most effective methods for assessing your new workplace environment, as coworkers may be eager to tell you about their work experiences. Be sure to avoid approaching your coworkers in a way that appears like you are seeking office gossip. For example, if you approach your coworkers intending to find the most responsible workers in the office, you risk offending someone. Be sure to frame all questions in a thoughtful

---

[1] Kendra Cherry, "The Norm of Reciprocity: When Someone Does Something Nice, Most People Want to Return the Favor," Verywell Mind, last modified September 11, 2018, https://www.verywellmind.com/what-is-the-rule-of-reciprocity-2795891.

and diplomatic manner. Review the following examples of questions you might ask your coworkers:

- ✔ **"What can I do to impress a certain manager?"** This question establishes you as a highly motivated employee. This question also elicits specific information, which may be easily applied in your workplace transition.

- ✔ **"What should I do if I need more time to complete a project?"** This question enables you to determine additional options, which may relieve you of unnecessary stress related to new deadlines.

- ✔ **"What time does everyone arrive for work in the mornings?"** This question defines normal behavior in your workplace, without expressing personal judgments or expectations.

- ✔ **"Do people usually leave on time at the end of the day, or do they stay later?"** This question also elicits the normal behavior among coworkers in your new workplace, without expressing any personal judgments or expectations.

- ✔ **"Who should I seek for assistance with a certain project?"** This question enables you to identify helpful resources in your new workplace.

At first, you might think these questions are too simple to uncover a great deal of useful information about your new workplace environment. However, you should in fact be aiming for simplicity. You do not want your colleagues to perceive you as brash with your line of questioning, as you are also attempting to establish positive relationships with them. Pressing your coworkers with a series of demanding questions may be rude, and may sour any chance at successful first impressions.

Review the following examples of questions you should avoid asking your coworkers:

- ✗ **"What is the best way to get a promotion?"** This question may make your coworkers hesitant to answer, as they themselves might be pursuing the same promotions that are of interest to you. Instead of this question, ask how you can provide the utmost service to the workplace. This replacement question assuages any fears amongst your colleagues that you are more interested in a promotion than being a reliable team member.

- ✗ **"Who is the best worker in the office?"** Your coworkers might be offended by this question's brash nature. They may also want to name themselves as the best employee, or they might refuse to name anyone. Either way, this question might result in hurt feelings while earning you a reputation for being impolitely straightforward.

- ✗ **"Who is the biggest jerk in the office?"** The temptation to ask about the office "jerk" or "ice queen" can be alluring for some readers. After all, you would undoubtedly prefer to avoid nasty encounters with an unfriendly employee or overly demanding manager. Resist the temptation to ask questions like this one, as they risk establishing you as the ringleader of an office gossip circle.

By asking the right questions and being friendly to your coworkers, you will gain access to a great deal of valuable information about your office environment with little personal cost.

Observe Your Workplace

Asking thoughtful questions will provide you with critical insight into your new workplace environment, but do not

CHAPTER 3: Adjust to Your Workplace Environment

forget to utilize your own observations. Watch your workplace for details that your coworkers might not mention. Use the following techniques to assess the hidden secrets of your workplace:

- [ ] **Observe employees who consistently deliver projects on time and within budget.** These are the employees who can provide the most valuable insights on how to complete tasks in your new workplace. Consider how they approach specific tasks, the amount of time they spend on their work, and who they consult for advice. Also observe how they prepare for presentations, speak to clients, and delegate tasks. This process may feel like the work of an investigative journalist, and your observations could reap serious benefits.

- [ ] **Note how different behaviors are rewarded or rebuked within the office.** For example, if your manager rewards team leaders rather than all team employees, seek out leadership responsibilities in order to establish yourself as a proficient and valuable employee. When you have a more definitive idea of your workplace's preferred behaviors, model yourself to exhibit these behaviors. This analysis will also help you discern which traits tend to go unnoticed by supervisors and management.

- [ ] **Examine how your coworkers are disciplined.** By noting the consequences of missing deadlines or displaying ineffective workplace behaviors, you will better understand your workplace's perspective on risk-taking. If you notice your workplace takes a more relaxed approach to discipline—for example, if employees rarely receive verbal warnings—then your workplace probably encourages relevant risk-taking behaviors. However, if your manager administers stern discipline, your workplace probably does not approve of risk-taking. Notice how your fellow employees are disciplined, then adjust your behavior accordingly so you are not forced to discover your company's disciplinary approach the hard way.

Observe Your Coworkers in Meetings

When you participate in meetings with your manager and fellow employees, observe how your coworkers behave. For example, notice if your coworkers speak in a casual manner, or if they speak deliberately and formally. Note if meetings are conducted with meticulous rules and regulations, or if they flow naturally like creative brainstorming sessions. Finally, notice how your coworkers and managers dress for the meeting. Your meeting's degree of formality and adherence to rules should give you a strong idea of how to act.

When you understand how to behave within your workplace environment, you can give more careful consideration to developing positive and beneficial relationships with your coworkers.

Demonstrate Basic Office Manners

At first, you might struggle to see any connection between office manners and your status as a proficient and highly valued employee. However, it is important to consider office manners within the framework of your workplace environment. For example, if you frequently eat odorous foods at your cubicle, your coworkers may resent you for failing to be considerate of your peers. This resentment might needlessly complicate the process of establishing positive and honest relationships with your coworkers, and thereby communicate to your supervisor that you are not a team player.

Even the smallest lapse in basic office manners can negatively impact your value in your workplace. When you behave in a polite and kind manner with your colleagues, you strengthen your professional reputation while increasing your

CHAPTER 3: Adjust to Your Workplace Environment

likelihood of receiving kind treatment in return. Use the following techniques to develop your office manners and improve your reputation within the workplace:

☐ **Greet everyone with a kind word.** If you are in the middle of work, a smile and a head nod will suffice.

☐ **Respect your colleagues' conversations.** Avoid interrupting your peers when they are conversing with each other. This is particularly important during meetings, as interrupting your colleagues will demonstrate a lack of interest in what others say. Active listening is a valuable skill to demonstrate to your managers, and it also minimizes the possibility of miscommunication.

☐ **Refrain from frequently interrupting your colleagues with emails or phone calls.** If you require urgent attention from a colleague, speak to him or her in person. Knock on your colleague's door and ask if he or she has time to speak before listing your reasons for interrupting.

☐ **Obtain permission before using anything that belongs to a coworker.** For example, if you innocently borrow a notepad, your coworker might lose the crucial information for a work project contained in it. Asking for permission is a simple demonstration of respect for your coworkers and their belongings.

☐ **Avoid eating odorous foods in your workplace.** Food smells are often pervasive, and they may cause your coworkers to lose focus on their work.

☐ **Maintain communal spaces.** Do not leave messes in the break room. Clean your space after meetings, and avoid leaving smelly foods in the break room's refrigerator, as this might offend your coworkers.

☐ **If you listen to music while working, keep your volume low so that your fellow coworkers cannot hear it.** Music can be distracting to your coworkers, so be polite by keeping your music to yourself. Depending on the proximity of your coworkers, you may need to wear headphones. If so, take precautions to ensure you do not isolate yourself from your nearby peers.

In addition to the above demonstrations of admirable office manners, remember to avoid spreading gossip, as this is can curtail workplace productivity and belittle your perceived value as a well-mannered employee.

Develop Rapport with Colleagues

Your coworkers are instrumental in successfully adjusting to your workplace and establishing yourself as a proficient and valuable employee. However, there is a difference between being a great friend with a coworker and having a positive and productive work relationship with them. Although being friends with a coworker might be entertaining, your friendship might not necessarily add to your value as an employee. In fact, if you and a small group of employees have a clique-like attitude towards interacting with other coworkers, your workplace friendships might be detrimental to your productivity. Managers place great value on employees that work well with others, so participating in a clique may undermine your efforts to improve your standing in the company.

Positive relationships with coworkers are built on honesty and trust. If your peers believe you are dishonestly acting nice for the purpose of securing a promotion, your relationships will be unstable. In order to establish excellent relationships with your coworkers and truly work well with your peers, utilize the following techniques:

☐ **Learn your colleagues' names as soon as possible.** While memorizing names is challenging for some employees, anyone can learn and master this skill with practice. When you are introduced to a new colleague, say his or her name aloud during the introduction. When you have a moment to yourself, physically write that person's name alongside any characteristics or descriptions that aid in anchoring that colleague's name in your memory.

- [ ] **Socialize with your coworkers.** Coffee runs and team lunches are great opportunities to get to know your colleagues on a personal level, which makes for a great foundation for positive professional relationships. Remember to keep office gossip to a minimum and never become too rowdy during a team happy hour.

- [ ] **Treat your colleagues with the degree of respect you expect to receive from them.**

- [ ] **Never yell at another employee.** Regardless of how justified you believe you might be, productive work becomes a hopeless task when you yell at your colleagues.

- [ ] **If a crisis occurs at work, relax before you react.** Impulsive reactions stem from your emotions, which may not always be productive. If your colleagues see you are constantly stressed and frustrated by your work, they might avoid talking with you altogether.

- [ ] **If you make a mistake, apologize immediately**. Ask your coworkers to let you know how you can amend the error. Immediately making an apology establishes you as a reliable and mature employee.

Establishing honest and productive relationships with your colleagues revolves about being kind and respectful. Keep your coworkers in mind when engaging in certain behaviors around the office.

Develop Rapport with Managers

Successfully adjusting to your workplace environment also depends on your ability to maintain positive relationships with

CHAPTER 3: Adjust to Your Workplace Environment

your managers. Your manager may be searching for employees who are willing to volunteer for tasks, are calm in intense situations, and are consistently dependable. While you might fit all these criteria, you might nonetheless find it difficult to communicate your value and relevant skills when you do not have an excellent relationship with your manager. By establishing excellent relationships with your supervisors, you will find more opportunities to communicate your value and proficiency.

The ability to establish a desirable relationship with your manager depends largely upon your standing as an employee. When you prove to your manager that you are capable of meeting deadlines and handling whatever projects he or she assigns you, that manager will perceive you as an effective employee. Use the following tips to establish respectful and beneficial relationships with your managers:

☐ **Always arrive on time.** Regardless of how effectively and thoroughly you complete your tasks throughout the day, your manager will not consider you reliable if he or she cannot trust you to arrive when the work day begins.

☐ **Volunteer for projects which your manager might find unpleasant.** You do not always need to volunteer for grunt work; however, when you demonstrate to your manager that you are willing to assist with challenging administrative tasks, he or she will appreciate your work and view you more favorably.

☐ **Demonstrate your abilities to thrive in both individual work and group work settings.** Compliment your fellow coworkers when they suggest excellent ideas at meetings. Volunteer to lead a few projects, or suggest another coworker who would be great leading a team during a particular task in a project. By knowing when to distinguish yourself and when to "share the spotlight" with others, you balance being both a team leader and a team player.

CHAPTER 3: Adjust to Your Workplace Environment

- [ ] **Display your problem-solving abilities.** One of the best ways to establish a positive relationship with your manager is by demonstrating your abilities to find solutions to work problems. Resist the temptation to ask your supervisor for directions unless absolutely necessary. Instead, brainstorm potential solutions before discussing the problem with your boss. Your supervisor will be impressed by your ability to solve problems on your own.

- [ ] **Showcase your hard work.** Do not brag about your accomplishments at the company; instead, tactfully mention to your manager how you have successfully solved a problem that had been previously plaguing the workplace. This expression allows you to highlight your hard work and value without sounding self-absorbed.

- [ ] **Request projects or tasks to volunteer for.** If there are currently no projects or tasks available to volunteer for, knock on your supervisor's door or send a friendly email asking if there are any projects you can help with. Making this gesture solidifies your reputation as a team player and reliable employee.

- [ ] **Be loyal to your manager.** No matter how much work your supervisors have assigned you, resist the temptation to complain to another employee. These complaints might be repeated or overheard by your supervisor. Furthermore, failing to be genuine with both your coworkers and your managers can undermine your reputation for honesty.

- [ ] **Avoid becoming overly friendly with your manager.** Regardless of how much you have in common, becoming overly friendly with a supervisor crosses a professional boundary. Be amicable with your boss, but be sure to omit unprofessional information, such as the details of your last drunken night out or your weekend antics at a friend's bachelor party. Allow your manager to lead with topics so you do not accidentally share inappropriate information.

☐ **Seek honest feedback from your manager.** When you ask for feedback regarding your job performance, your manager will perceive you as an employee who is genuinely concerned with performing his or her job as well as possible.

☐ **When appropriate, seek needed face-to-face time with your company's leaders.** Avoid interrupting your managers with personal questions and concerns. Instead, select a time at which you know they will be available, then offer to get coffee with your boss or discuss relevant issues while transitioning back to work after a break.

☐ **If your manager asks you a question that you do not know the answer to, let him or her know you will happily find the answer as soon as possible.** Do not simply shrug your shoulders and say, "I don't know." For example, if your manager asks you what it would cost to hire a certain supplier, inform him or her that you will be researching this cost during your first opportunity. Then, when you do, immediately send your manager an email with an answer to the question.

Establishing positive and beneficial relationships with your managers relies heavily upon your abilities to produce excellent work and meet project deadlines. These productive work behaviors inform your managers that they can rely on you to handle excess work they might find overwhelming, which establishes you as a proficient employee in your workplace.

Use Technology Appropriately

In today's technologically advanced workplace, smartphones, email, and other digital assets play a critical role in your ability to perform your job. You may need to be in constant contact with your manager via cell phone, or you may be required to communicate with a client across the world via email or videoconferencing software. Given modern technology's level of integration within daily job activities, you must approach technology with the best behavior possible. Misuse of technology—whether intentional or accidental—could result in disciplinary action from your manager. The following two example scenarios demonstrate how misused technology can cause trouble for employees:

***

Example #1: Matt

Matt is a product director responsible for interfacing with clients who send questions via an online messaging platform. Matt's chats with prospective clients are typically saved within his work email so he can present any leads to the company's sales team. Matt is attending a bachelor party in a few weeks, and he is responsible for making reservations for the group. Matt orders a party bus and makes reservations to several clubs during his lunch hour, using his work email for reservation confirmation. Later, while forwarding work-related emails to his sales team, he accidentally sends one pertaining to his friend's bachelor party. Matt's boss gives him a stern verbal warning, reminding him that using work email for personal activities is strictly prohibited.

***

Example #2: Julia

Julia is an assistant who is given a smartphone by the company to use for work purposes. Her boss typically communicates with her via text message outside of work hours. One night, Julia is out with friends when her boss sends her a text asking that she come in early the next day. Julia is frustrated by the request, as she knows she will only get a few hours of sleep. She types a text message intended for her

CHAPTER 3: Adjust to Your Workplace Environment

husband in which she complains about her boss, then accidentally sends it back to her boss. While Julia is not directly penalized for using the phone for personal use, her manager becomes distant and dismissive with her, and she is overlooked for future project opportunities.

***

As the above two examples demonstrate, mishandled technology can undermine any worker's efforts to become a proficient employee. You must use your best behavior when dealing with any work phones, emails, or other technologies related to your job. Employ the following techniques when using modern technology on the job:

☐ **Gain a clear understanding of your company's policies regarding technology use on the job.** This information can typically be found in your employee handbook. Ask your manager for clarity if you are still uncertain about any policies.

☐ **Resist the temptation to use your work email for personal tasks.** Sending digital confirmations for shopping orders to your work email address may be alluring, but many companies monitor employee email, so always act accordingly.

☐ **Refrain from using the internet for personal tasks when you are on company time.** While working, forego the online shopping, social media, or online chatting. The loss of reputation from being caught idly browsing the web is difficult to recover from, so avoid this situation at all costs.

☐ **Use company phones for work only.** Do not use this device for personal texts or phone calls to friends or family members. Many companies monitor the use of work phones, so always act accordingly. Stay on your best

CHAPTER 3: Adjust to Your Workplace Environment

behavior to avoid any complicated situations regarding misuse of technology.

If you are caught using technology for personal use in the workplace, apologize immediately and do not do it again. Your manager may forgive an innocent mistake if you are quick to admit your error in judgement. However, if your manager catches you misusing company technology a second time, he or she may assume you are wasting a large portion of your work time with unrelated activities such as shopping or chatting online.

Adjusting to your workplace environment can be challenging, especially if you are transitioning into a new environment entirely different from your previous job or position. However, the techniques contained within this chapter will help you quickly surpass this transitional stage and establish yourself as a proficient employee.

In the next chapter, we will explore how you might establish yourself in your workplace environment by confidently making decisions and solving problems.

CHAPTER 4

How to Make Decisions and Solve Problems

We make decisions every day. We decide which road to take when we commute to work; we decide what time to wake up in the morning; we decide what to eat for breakfast. Decision making is so heavily woven into our lives that we seldom realize how many decisions we make throughout the course of a single day. With each decision, our brains evaluate our situations and compare tangible outcomes to achieve the optimal results. Even seemingly small decisions, like what we choose to put in our coffee, can send our brains buzzing.

As an employee, you are expected to make several decisions throughout the course of the average work day—many of which will have a profound impact on your responsibilities and your organization itself. Although making decisions offers you opportunities to demonstrate your value as an employee, these instances might sometimes feel like debilitating experiences, especially when the decisions in question are rather daunting.

For example, suppose your manager leaves you responsible for a project team. This is your first time leading a group of fellow employees, and you are thrilled at the opportunity. Your manager gives you full control, including the ability to make crucial budget decisions. During the process of completing this project, your team members approach you with a dilemma: they need an expensive tool to ensure high-quality results for the project, but the tool in question cannot be found in the budget. In this scenario, your choices are obvious:

- **Option #1:** You will buy the expensive tool and hope the investment is worthwhile in the long term,
- **Option #2:** You will continue to use the tools you have been given and produce a lesser-quality outcome that might not impress your manager.

How will you decide? Decision making is essentially understanding every option available to you, gathering the necessary information for arriving at a conclusion, and creating an action plan for remaining accountable and tracking your progress. When you have mastered these techniques, you will be equipped to handle nearly any problem that appears in your workplace. An employee capable of making rational decisions with confidence and ease is an employee who will be truly valued by his or her managers.

Understand the Entire Problem

At first, making decisions within your workplace might be intimidating, especially if your work environment is particularly fast paced. Remember that humans are naturally endowed with the ability to make careful and rational decisions. Our brains are engineered to solve a range of perplexing problems.

Before we dive into the "how to" of decision making, let us consider how the brain reacts when it encounters challenges that require informed decisions. Understanding how the brain makes decisions can offer valuable insight into how we can make more effective and rational choices. Studies have revealed two components of the brain's decision making system: the neocortex, which is associated with short-term memory and slow, logical, and conscious thought processes; and the limbic system, which is associated with long-term memory and quick, primal, emotional connections to pain,

CHAPTER 4: Make Decisions and Solve Problems

pleasure, past successes, and past failures.[2] These two components might feel like opposing forces: the neocortex decides by slowly analyzing facts, while the limbic system decides in the form of immediate "gut" reactions. If you have ever found yourself in the middle of a junk food aisle at a grocery store, you know exactly what this internal struggle feels like. Your rational brain understands the health benefits of buying more wholesome foods, but your neurons may be firing in favor of a candy bar in front of you. If you have a difficulty making decisions that favor long-term rewards, scientists might conclude that your brain is unable to differentiate between risk and reward.

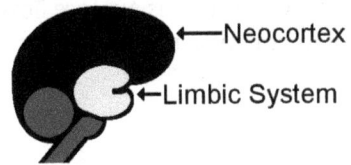

Decision making, like other proficiency skills, is learnable. Deciphering the science behind decision making can help explain why you may be initially prone to some behaviors. The techniques and strategies in this chapter are designed to help you desert negative habits and instead embrace skills that make you a valuable part of your workplace community.

The key to harnessing your natural decision-making power is understanding how to encourage your ability to rationally assess your options and make the ideal selection based on the information currently available to you. Individuals with exceptional decision-making and problem-solving skills also make every effort to minimize emotions and other conflicting factors that could distort their judgments. An employee's goal must be to make informed

---

[2] Roy Wood and Patrick Barker, "'This is Your Brain...' A Decision-Making Machine," *Defense Acquisition Research Journal* 15, no. 3 (November–December 2015): 61–63.

and educated decisions that offer the greatest benefits for the organization.

Returning to our previous example, the dilemma of whether or not to purchase the expensive tool that cannot be found in the budget, you might be tempted to take a risk and invest in the more expensive tool. However, the rational decision might be remaining within the original budget, or cutting costs elsewhere and thereby allowing for the costly tool without exceeding the budget.

Not all decisions can be made easily, especially if they are intended to address complex problems. Therefore, you must do everything you can to prepare yourself for the decision-making and problem-solving processes. Let us explore how to carefully analyze information for making the best decisions possible.

Gather Information about the Problem

Think back to high school English class, when you were about to write a paper. The first step you were always told to take, before you even put your pen to paper, was to research your topic. Successful decision making also involves a great deal of research, especially when the decision has a profound impact on a work project or process. By researching everything involved in the dilemma, you will have all the information you need to make an informed decision. Use the following research techniques:

☐ **Refer to important people for guidance.** Let us return again to the dilemma of whether or not to purchase the expensive tool. You may be tempted to invest in it, as your team members predict the decision will produce high-quality project outcomes. However, the person whose opinion should be your highest priority is the manager who gave you responsibility of the work team. Asking questions does not reflect poorly on your value as a team leader. Leaders are not afraid to ask for guidance, especially if guidance is necessary for making an informed and rational decision.

- [ ] **Ask for necessary information.** In the previous dilemma of whether or not to purchase the expensive tool, you might refer to your manager for advice on the appropriate steps to take. However, to truly enhance your decision making abilities, avoid asking the manager to make the decision for you. Instead, ask your manager to provide you with information needed for you to make your own decision. Your manager might inform you that overspending will put other organizational projects at risk, or that reducing spending on other items in the budget will undermine the overall quality of the project.

- [ ] **Make decisions independently.** By using the technique described above, you will gain necessary information from your manager without appearing incapable of making the decision yourself. Strengthening your decision-making skills requires making choices on your own, not asking others to make them for you.

✖ "What should I do?"

✔ "Can you provide any additional information for me to consider when making this decision?"

- [ ] **Brainstorm with others to ensure you completely understand what the decision involves.** For example, if you are tasked with creating a project budget, ask the project team members what resources, tools, and materials they need for the project. This way, you will have a complete understanding of the dilemma, which can help you choose the most appropriate solution.

- [ ] **Refer to your favorite search engine for the information you might need.** Third-party research can be incredibly valuable in the decision-making process, so look to outside information if you need some assistance. For example, if you are an office manager and you must decide which new equipment needs to be installed in the workplace, consider searching consumer reviews to determine the best value. When you are more informed of your potential choices, you will be more likely to make the optimal decision.

☐ **Review case studies or news articles that resemble your situation.** For example, if your manager wants to shorten the allotted lunch break time by 15 minutes, search online to research companies who have already enacted similar policies. Gathering data will help solidify and support your decision. In this case, you will probably explain to your manager that employees who have shorter lunch times are generally less engaged and less productive during afternoon work hours.[3] Research will help you make an educated decision, which is essential to becoming a highly valued employee.

☐ **Ask a friend or family member to assess your problem and decision.** Oftentimes our loved ones can provide us with an objective opinion of a situation at work, as they are separated from office politics or personal hesitations. Unless disclosing certain company information undermines a confidentiality clause, ask a knowledgeable friend or family member for their opinion regarding your decision.

---

[3] Alan Kohll, "New Study Shows Correlation Between Employee Engagement And The Long-Lost Lunch Break," Forbes, last modified May 29, 2018, https://www.forbes.com/sites/alankohll/2018/05/29/new-study-shows-correlation-between-employee-engagement-and-the-long-lost-lunch-break/#5eb7b2de4efc.

CHAPTER 4: Make Decisions and Solve Problems

Compare Your Options

Confident and rational decisions cannot be made unless you understand every choice available to you. Talk to your fellow employees, managers, and team members to ensure you have full comprehension of all available options.

If you need to make an urgent decision and you do not have time for consulting other people, set aside 10 to 20 minutes of your time to brainstorm. Turn off your phone and email notifications, then relocate to a quiet area where you will not be disturbed; distractions are detrimental to this process. When you have eliminated all distractions, write all the potential decisions that you could make to solve your problem. Do not waste time debating whether each possible solution is feasible; instead, write them as soon as they enter your mind. When you have filled a page or two with potential decisions, analyze each of your solutions to assess their viabilities. If you have trouble with this process, consider outlining your desired outcome. Ask yourself the following questions for each of your recorded options to determine if it could successfully serve as the ideal decision:

- Can I undertake this option in the amount of time I have available?
- Is this a decision that my company can implement without straining budgets, resources, etc.?
- Do I have the necessary knowledge and skills to follow through with this decision?
- Does this lead to my desired outcome?

By answering the above questions, you create a shortlist of potential decisions that have a high probability of leading to a favorable outcome. After generating this shortlist, begin selecting the best decision to solve your problem.

Examine Your Hunches

No examination of decision making and problem solving would be complete without considering "hunches." You know what they feel like: gut instincts that urge you to make certain decisions even if you lack information to defend them. Hunches are usually our instincts' way of letting us know what decision to make, as our brains subconsciously collect enough information to arrive at conclusions on their own.

You should not always trust your hunches, as they might easily be mistaken for emotional reactions. If you are approaching a decision with a strong emotion, you are more likely to make a poor choice, as your emotions might blind you to information that is relevant to the decision.

There are certain strategies you can use to determine the difference between a helpful hunch and a destructive emotional reaction, then make use of hunches to supplement your decision-making process. These strategies include the following:

- [ ] **Ask for feedback about your hunch.** Consider grabbing lunch with a knowledgeable coworker or meeting with your manager to talk about the decision. Getting validation for your hunch is not always necessary to the decision-making process, but it provides valuable objectivity.

- [ ] **If you experience an unsettling feeling about a certain decision, write why you feel this way.** When you start processing your hunch and articulating it in words, you might discover a coherent decision that your mind already made before you realized it.

- [ ] **If you immediately feel compelled to take a certain course of action when a problem is presented to you, you are experiencing an emotional reaction.** Hunches develop slowly, as your brain needs time to subconsciously process all information relevant to the problem. Immediate and emotional reactions to a problem are typically based on "fight-or-flight" responses, and are unproductive for decision making.

Hunches can be a valuable part of the decision-making process, but only if they are used appropriately. When you have articulated your hunch in words, follow the tips and techniques described earlier in this chapter to determine whether or not it is viable. This assessment will provide you with the necessary information to defend your hunch should other employees or managers question the rationale behind your decision.

Sleep on It

The brain absorbs a great deal of information throughout the day, which often leaves it clouded by constant stimuli. Research has demonstrated that while sleeping, our brains constantly look for solutions to problems.[4] Furthermore, many researchers believe the solutions we discover while asleep are often the ideal option. This is due to a phenomenon known as "unconscious processing," by which our brains collect and analyze every piece of information we have been exposed to throughout the day. Though you may be asleep, your brain is busy using all its available information to subconsciously solve the problems that plague you throughout the day. You may recognize this process from instances where you have gone to sleep stressed about a dilemma, only to wake up with a firm resolution of your next course of action.

The time we spend sleeping is a mentally active period, during which the brain assesses and connects seemingly unassociated information to determine the best choice in a dilemma. Use the following tips to sleep better and take advantage of your unconscious processing:

---

[4] Ut Na Sio, Padraic Monaghan, and Tom Ormerod, "Sleep on It, but Only If It is Difficult: Effects of Sleep on Problem Solving," *Memory & Cognition* 41, no. 2 (February 2013): 159–166.

☐ **Find the perfect amount of sleep for your body.** Most people need about eight hours of sleep each night, though some individuals need less and others need even more. Experiment with your sleeping time until you wake feeling refreshed and revitalized. Consider going to sleep 15 minutes earlier each night until you wake feeling completely rested. Keep a sleep log by taking note of how many hours you sleep each night and how you feel when you wake in the morning. See the following example of a sleep log:

CHAPTER 4: Make Decisions and Solve Problems

Date	Went to Bed	Woke Up	Total Sleep Time	Feeling
1/1	1:00 AM	7:00 AM	6:00	Exhausted
1/2	11:30 PM	6:00 AM	6:30	Tired
1/3	11:00 PM	7:00 AM	8:00	Rested

For additional assistance in creating your sleep log, see the following template:

CHAPTER 4: Make Decisions and Solve Problems

Date	Went to Bed	Woke Up	Total Sleep Time	Feeling

☐ **Minimize the technology arranged in your bedroom.** Studies show that the light emitted from your television, computer, and phone inhibits melatonin production, thereby keeping you awake longer.[5] Even red light from a digital alarm clock might interfere with a good night's sleep. Turn off all technology about an hour before you go to bed to increase melatonin production and fall asleep faster. Also consider searching for software that adjusts the color temperature of your computer screen display to minimize its effect on your sleep patterns.

☐ **Use a white noise machine to minimize noise that might wake you through the night.** Consider investing in your sleep by purchasing a white noise machine to minimize sounds like street traffic or boisterous roommates. These devices produce a gentle and relaxing sound that will lull you into a deep sleep. White noise machines aid in falling asleep faster and preventing you from being prematurely woken, which are vital components of unlocking your brain's decision-making abilities.

Commit to getting the eight hours of sleep necessary for making effective workplace decisions. Consider sleep as important as a meeting with your manager or that looming deadline, so you will be less likely to blow it off.

Build Confidence in Your Decision

After you have gathered the necessary information to solve a problem, you must implement your decision without wasting time worrying if it was an appropriate choice. If you used all

---

[5] Matthias Bues, Achim Pross, Oliver Stefani, Silvia Frey, Doreen Anders, Jakub Spati, Anna Wirz-Justice, Ralph Mager, and Christian Cajochen, "LED-Backlit Computer Screens Influence Our Biological Clock and Keep Us More Awake." *Journal of the Society for Information Display* 20, no. 5 (May 2012): 266–272, https://doi.org/10.1889/jsid20.5.266.

the tips from this section, you will be on your way to a successful outcome; however, acting on a decision is not always easy.

Procrastination is often a sign of insecurity about your ability to see a decision through to its outcome. Some people agonize over making the "right" decision to the degree that they miss their opportunity, and they never act at all. Of course, doing nothing is always an option itself. Sometimes doing nothing may even turn out to be the best option, though decisive and effective action is often most desirable.

There is a trend known as "paralysis of analysis" where too many factors are weighed too frequently as people try to consider every possible outcome.[6] Acting upon a decision takes a degree of courage because risk is always involved. The decision, no matter how carefully weighed, may be affected by factors that unexpectedly enter the situation.

For example, you might hesitate to implement a certain decision because you are worried about failing. This is probably the most common reason people avoid acting on decisions, especially for employees who seek recognition as a valuable member of the workplace. However, you must realize that no businessperson—even among Fortune 500 CEOs—is perfect. Mistakes are a natural aspect of growth and, while hardly pleasant, they teach lessons that lead to professional and personal achievements. To act on a decision with confidence, even if you are feeling extremely nervous, consider implementing the following techniques:

☐ **Visualize the future where the decision has been made and implemented.** Consider every single detail, including how you will feel after you take action, what you will be doing when the decision is underway, etc.

---

[6] Amir Sharif, "Paralysis by Analysis? The Dilemma of Choice and the Risks of Technology Evaluation." *Journal of Enterprise Information Management* 21, no. 1 (2007): 8–12, https://doi.org/10.1108/17410390810842291.

Answer the following questions to further specify your future after acting on the decision:

- What does the workplace look like?
- What does the future feel like?
- What will happen in your role once you have acted on the decision?
- What will you do once the decision has been implemented and concluded?

There are no limits when it comes to visualizing your future—in fact, when you supply and focus on more details, you will be better equipped for taking action.

☐ **Believe in the future.** In order to act on a decision, you need to truly believe you will achieve the best outcome. If you do not believe in your ability complete your objective in its entirety, you might procrastinate and ultimately sabotage your decision-making process.

☐ **Imagine the worst-case scenario aloud.** For example, when you drive home from work, talk aloud about what could happen when you implement your decision. Be as dramatic as possible. This will help you to realize that regardless of how badly the decision unfolds, your worst-case scenario is unlikely to happen. When you verge into outright fantasy ("I will get fired, blacklisted from the industry, and end up a loser"), verbally stop yourself and laugh at how ludicrous your worst-case scenario seems. Humor will give you a realistic perspective of your decision, which is critical to avoiding procrastination and stress.

After you have reminded yourself that your worst-case scenario is unlikely, consciously build the confidence necessary for implementing your decision, then take concrete actions throughout the implementation process.

CHAPTER 4: Make Decisions and Solve Problems

Implement Your Decision

Outline the potential barriers to your solution, the resources necessary to implement your decision, and the due dates for each of these actions. Many employees fail to follow through with their decisions because they do not allow for transparency and responsibility. To counteract this, plan exactly what is needed to implement your decision, including alternative methods. This level of precision will allow you to regularly review your progress.

Detail Your Decision in Small Action Steps

You will benefit from the tangible successes that these smaller action steps generate. For example, if you made the decision to create an office budget, break down this goal into smaller action steps. One step might include identifying spending limits for each department every three days. Not only will smaller steps aid in achieving larger goals, but they will provide a sense of accomplishment and the motivation you need for fully implementing your decision.

> Create an office budget (Action Steps):
> 1. Determine monthly income
> 2. Determine fixed costs
> 3. Include variable costs
> 4. Predict one-time expenditures
> 5. Build spreadsheet with above data
> 6. Make a new spending plan
> 7. Compare actual spending with new plan weekly
> 8. Adjust budget as necessary

Ensure All Relevant People Have the Plan

If there are several people involved in your decision-making process, create an action plan and provide it to all relevant people via email or printed notice. For example, if you are

Commit to One Decision

When all other decision implementation strategies fail, simply close your eyes, take a deep breath, and immediately commit to acting on one decision. This method is designed to prevent you from being paralyzed by excessive preparation. People will often conduct extraneous research and analysis as a form of procrastination, especially when they are insecure about their abilities to make a decision. While they hope their research might boost their confidences, they never make any progress.

Excessive preparation causes decision-making stagnation, as you might never feel ready to implement the decision. To counteract this effect, prepare a deadline by which you will make a decision and act upon it, regardless of how unprepared you might feel. When the decision's actions have been implemented, you can adjust plans as necessary—so long as you stop procrastinating and begin to act.

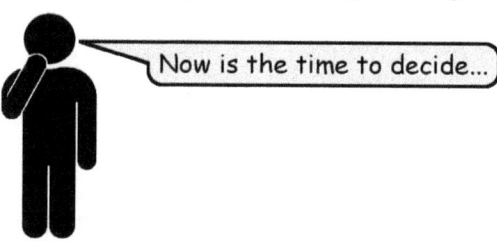

Review the Impact of Your Decision

After you have made a choice and acted upon it, complete the worthwhile practice of reflecting upon your decision so that you can make better-informed decisions in the future. Assess

CHAPTER 4: Make Decisions and Solve Problems

whether the decision ultimately brought about the intended result. If the decision did not produce the desired outcomes, you must determine why it did not work. Assess what aspect of your decision-making process went wrong, then learn from this mistake for future reference. Consider asking other employees or your manager for opinions, as other perspectives will help you to understand where you erred in your decision making.

Also reflect on decisions you have made over your entire life. While many of these decisions will be unrelated to business, they are nonetheless evidence of your decision-making style. Consider the decisions you have made and whether, in hindsight, you feel they were good or bad. These might be big or small decisions, such as what school to apply to, what job to take, or what car to purchase. Examining your decision-making processes for both professional and personal situations will provide insight into your decision-making style and successes.

You have undoubtedly made sound decisions in your life. Consider the factors that helped you make these decisions and the methods you used to make them. This reflective practice will give you valuable clues as to how you have made decisions and what tools you have used during your past successes. Trust yourself. Apply lessons from both this book and your own life to the process of becoming a more proficient employee.

If you made a decision that failed based on unforeseen circumstances, forgive yourself. One failure does not mean you are a bad decision maker; it simply means you encountered bad luck. Few experts accurately foresaw the mortgage meltdown or the Great Recession of 2008. For all their expertise, most economists, experts in the housing market, loan officers, bankers, government officials, and politicians did not predict the crash and did not know how to prevent it.

In your lifetime you have undoubtedly made numerous strong decisions; analyze them to understand what worked. At the same time, analyze your poor decisions to diagnose any errors that you should avoid in the future. As you assess these decisions, be kind to yourself. Nobody can foresee everything, and no employee makes perfect decisions every time.

Review Progress Whenever Possible

By reviewing progress and renewing commitment to your actions, you will ensure that the decision-making process maintains momentum. Additionally, you will provide yourself with much needed self-assurance. Noting progress at certain milestones will keep you prepared to enact the overall decision. Ask yourself the following questions at each milestone to review your progress toward your decision:

- Is this decision working for you? For the company? What key factors are responsible for this?

- If the decision is not working, what are the contributing factors for this outcome?

- What have been the most successful components of the decision to date?

- How will you celebrate your successes?

- How will you handle any mishaps or missed milestones after implementing the decision?

Revisit Alternative Solutions as Needed

Sometimes your decisions will not go according to plan. If this happens, revisit the alternative solutions you identified before implementing your current decision. Alternatives are a critical aspect of problem solving, especially if the primary solution is later revealed to have undesirable consequences.

Ensure that you have enough viable alternatives available and ample information about each decision and its

CHAPTER 4: Make Decisions and Solve Problems

consequences. By consciously establishing viable alternatives and gathering information about them, you expand the scope of your potential choices. For example, suppose your business is struggling under a load of debt. In addition to the primary solution of increasing profits, you might consider alternative options such as selling assets to pay the debt or declaring bankruptcy.

A brainstorming session among people who are directly involved in the business could also yield positive alternatives which you may not have considered yourself. In the example above, an employee might suggest selling the business to a local competitor. Another employee might consider investing directly.

Brainstorming for alternative solutions involves putting all options "on the table" and considering each one in order to stimulate creative thinking. Returning to the previous example of your company struggling under a load of debt, if an employee suggests, "We could hold an expo down in Florida to try to recruit clients," the suggestion is treated seriously and written down as a possible alternative. The next employee's suggestion might be more realistic, but still stimulated by the previous one: "We could meet with one specific client that has already expressed interest in hopes of gaining a contract with the company."

After you have generated a list of alternatives, review the consequences each would have. For example, while selling company assets may be a great way to improve the company's bottom line in the short term, it could severely impact the company's ability to operate over the long term. Ideally, the best decision would have a positive impact in both long-term and short-term scenarios; however, do not allow these deliberations to prevent you from making a decision at all. Carefully analyze each of your alternative solutions to determine which one will have the greatest desired impact.

Accept Your Mistakes

Some decisions are not as straightforward as we might like. There will not always be favorable outcomes. In some instances, you might fail to identify a single feasible solution to a problem, especially if the issue in question is complex and impacts your entire workplace. When you encounter a seemingly unsolvable problem, do not judge yourself too critically. Avoid internalizing this temporary setback, as doing so might prevent you from achieving your career goals, or paralyze you from making future decisions. Instead, view this setback as a learning experience that not all problems are instantly solvable.

Remember, you are only human. Every person on the planet has made a poor decision. If you quickly recover from your mistakes and take more productive actions, you will not allow a single mistake to depress your career trajectory. Do not berate yourself if your decision-making process fails. Instead, continue to take actions which maintain your motivation and lead you to success. When you continuously demonstrate your ability to make solid decisions, you will solve short-term problems and also exemplify your value to your company.

In the next chapter, we will discover how you can enhance your performance by embracing the benefits of stress management.

CHAPTER 5

How to Embrace the Benefits of Stress Management

Stress is everywhere—and you have probably experienced your fair share of anxiety as well. Whether you are a single parent working to support your kids, a veteran looking to transition into the professional world, or simply an employee adjusting to new life changes, stress is a natural aspect of the modern lifestyle. Despite the normalcy of stress, it might be a difficult sensation to pin down. You probably know what stress feels like, but if you cannot recognize why it happens and how to deal with it, stress will significantly impair your job performance.

While normal stress levels are healthy and even motivational, an overwhelming amount of stress has a severe negative impact on your ability to provide value to your company. High levels of stress lead to damaging situations, such as the following:

- ✗ **You frequently become ill, which forces you to take sick days in order to recuperate.** This places you behind schedule for your projects, which might lead your managers to view you as unreliable. This unfair assessment might then contribute you your burden of stress, creating a vicious cycle that is difficult to break.

- ✗ **You lose the ability to concentrate on your work.** This leads to missed deadlines and low-quality performance, which significantly impacts your reputation as a valuable and dependable employee.

CHAPTER 5: Embrace the Benefits of Stress Management

× **You become moody and depressed.** This isolates you from your fellow employees, undermining your reputation as a team player.

A significant burden of stress is a massive hindrance to your ability to perform your job well, and ultimately detracts from your value to your company. Significant stress might cause you to produce low-quality work or become too depressed or anxious to serve as an effective team member. You must implement stress management within your own life, as it preserves your capacity to perform your job to the best of your abilities.

When you are feeling well rested, calm, and motivated, you are better suited to impress your manager by demonstrating your unique talents and abilities. In addition to these benefits, managing your stress will lead you to become a major inspiration to your fellow employees. Everyone will want to know the stress-busting secrets of the office's most levelheaded employee, and you will be looked to as a model employee within your workplace.

Understand Stress and Its Impact on You

Stress is our bodies' physical and emotional reactions to an external situation in our environment. Long ago, stress was vital to our ancestors' survival, as it urged them to either fight or flee from dangerous situations. The symptoms we experience when stressed—which include faster heartbeat, elevated blood pressure levels, and feelings of nervousness or excitement—have helped our species survive and thrive. Today, the physiological reaction of stress remains the same. However, our stimulators are very different than those which the early humans faced, and they keep us in a constant state of stress.

Despite the different levels and types of stress each professional may experience, the physiological symptoms are easily recognizable. Common symptoms of stress include the following:

- Prolonged elevated heart rates and palpitations
- Sweaty palms
- Headaches
- Dizziness
- Teeth grinding
- Twitching eyes and muscles
- Upset stomach
- Fatigue
- Sweating
- Muscle tension and stiffness
- Insomnia

CHAPTER 5: Embrace the Benefits of Stress Management

Stress might also manifest in certain mental and emotional reactions. We have all experienced stress and its impact on our mental and social health. Perhaps you snapped at another employee without meaning to, or maybe you experienced a bout of depression due to prolonged stress at work. Other mental and emotional symptoms of stress include the following:

- Depression
- Anxiety
- Worry
- Irritability
- Shortness of temper
- Absentmindedness
- Self-pity
- Social isolation

These common mental and emotional manifestations of stress seriously damage the quality of both your professional and personal lives. Consider the following two scenarios to understand how stress might manifest in individual cases, whether it is produced by work or at home:

***

Scenario #1: Sharon

Sharon is going through a messy divorce with her husband of 11 years. She works as an office manager for a mid-sized company that plans on moving to a larger location. As the office manager, Sharon is responsible for ensuring that all departments have a suitable workspace with all the tools and equipment they need. However, due to Sharon's recent divorce woes, she has trouble focusing at work. She stares blankly at her computer screen, cries at random intervals, and arrives to work looking less than ideal. While her managers understand the difficulties Sharon is experiencing, they worry she will not be able to handle the responsibilities associated with the company's upcoming move. As a result, they assign the primary responsibilities to a new administrative assistant, and eventually come to rely on him over Sharon for high-value tasks and projects.

***

Scenario #2: Chris

Chris is a paralegal working for a major law firm in metropolitan Boston. He recently moved to the city after graduating college and is having difficulty adjusting to these major life changes. In addition to finding a new apartment and starting payment on his student loans, he also has to deal with a new workplace culture that is extremely different from what he experienced in college. Chris finds himself unable to sleep at night and sometimes wakes up short of breath from stress-induced nightmares. Chris's lack of sleep reduces his ability to stay alert and motivated throughout the day, which is noticed by his supervisors. While Chris manages to adapt to his new situation after a few months, his supervisors remember his shaky acclimation period. As a result, Chris is later overlooked up for a valuable promotional opportunity.

***

In the above two scenarios, each employee has a different reason for suffering from significant amounts of stress. However, the result is ultimately the same: stress negatively impacts their abilities to do their work.

While there are certainly events where a profound impact on your job is unavoidable—for example, handling the death of a family member or caring for a sick child—employees must use expert stress management techniques to minimize the impact anxiety and personal strife have within their workplaces.

CHAPTER 5: Embrace the Benefits of Stress Management

Prevent and Relieve Stress

Before we examine some of the most effective stress management techniques, you must understand that not all strategies will be appropriate for everyone. People react to stressors in different ways, so people's stress management techniques will naturally vary in the same manner. Try as many techniques as possible to determine which solution suits you best.

While the most successful stress management strategies require an individualized approach for each person, the following techniques can provide comprehensive and insightful solutions to debilitating stress in a majority of cases. The stress solutions and coping strategies presented in this book were selected for the following reasons:

- They remedy the imbalance between negative and positive emotions
- They reduce harmful environmental stimuli
- They develop and maintain positive self-esteem
- They build satisfying and fulfilling relationships with others

Let us begin analyzing these beneficial stress management techniques now.

Organize Your Space

When you are continually surrounded by clutter throughout the work day, finding reports, keys, or other work necessities becomes a mentally taxing activity. Your mind tends to reflect the space around you. If your professional and personal spaces are kept organized, your mind will be more orderly and coordinated as well. If you have ever spent time in a tranquil spa or relaxing restaurant, you have probably noticed how these surroundings made you feel more peaceful. Apply the same principle to your workspace: if it is messy and cluttered, your mind will reflect your disorganized surroundings; but if it is open and organized, your mind will become more harmonious and coordinated. Use the following techniques to keep your space orderly and your mind free from scattered thoughts that instigate stress:

- [ ] **Clean your workspace.** You might be surprised by how much a clean desk and clutter-free workspace will calm you. This technique is especially useful if you know you will soon be facing a hectic deadline, and you need your surroundings to inspire a calm and relaxed attitude.

- [ ] **Sort through your files, documents, and any other paperwork stored at your desk.** Ask your supervisor for permission to move older documents to another workspace, such as an empty cubicle or storage room. If you cannot move these documents elsewhere, ask your supervisor for permission to scan the documents and store them digitally on your computer. This will reduce physical clutter while keeping the information easily accessible.

- [ ] **Make your workspace a place in which you enjoy working**. After you have cleaned your surroundings, ask your supervisor for permission to keep pictures of loved ones or a small colorful plant on your desk. These personal touches will make it easier for you to cheerfully complete your work on even the most stressful days. Be careful not to go to an extreme with decorations, as this recreates the sensation of having a cluttered desk. Also, realize your managers will not appreciate if you have covered your desk in holiday wrapping paper, or if you have enough plants to call your cubicle a garden.

Eat a Healthy Diet

When you find yourself working late or crunching to meet a tight deadline, the temptation to simply order out for pizza or fast food can be overwhelming. The reasoning behind this desire is simple: we assume that ordering delivery or eating a frozen dinner saves us valuable time and energy. You might even feel a sense of entitlement, as if you deserve to treat yourself for working so hard.

However, if you want to keep stress out of your life and stay focused on being a valuable and dependable employee, eat healthy. Maintaining a healthy diet will assist in fighting off sickness, and also aid you in staying alert and focused on your work. Recall the last time you had an unhealthy meal: you probably felt lethargic for a considerable amount of time afterwards. Eating multiple unhealthy meals in a row might turn this lethargy into a regular sensation, which may lead to mood swings and depression. When battling stress, your diet might make you into your own worst enemy. Turn yourself into an ally by using the following tips for eating healthy:

- [ ] **Pre-pack nutritious lunches to bring to work.** Ensure your lunches are filled with wholesome foods like a whole-wheat turkey sandwich, an apple, and a small bag of baked chips. Avoid bringing microwaveable meals, as these are loaded with sodium, and they fail to stave off hunger for more than a few hours.

- [ ] **Know which foods keep your energy up and your mind alert.** These snacks might include trail mix, sugar-free granola, or even pretzels. Keep these foods at your desk for when you start to feel sluggish or so stressed that you want to gorge on a cheeseburger. Be sure to eat an appropriate portion of these healthy snacks, as an entire bag of pretzels can be as bad for you as a bowl of ice cream.

Exercise Regularly

The benefits of exercise are profound, especially in regard to effective stress management. Research has confirmed that exercise reduces feelings of stress and anxiety.[7] Regular exercise will increase your overall health and provide you a sense of well-being, which will make you more positive in your daily life. To better understand why exercise should be an important part of your life, consider the following benefits:

- **Exercise releases your endorphins.** Physical activity helps your brain produce more endorphins, which are neurotransmitters that help you feel good. The more endorphins your brain produces, the better you feel.

- **Exercise improves your mood.** Regular physical activity benefits your self-confidence, even reducing the occurrence of symptoms commonly associated with depression and anxiety. Exercise also improves your sleep, which is another critical part of lowering your stress levels.

- **Exercise is meditation in motion**. After going for a jog around the block or taking a few laps in the pool, you may find that you have forgotten about the stresses of the day. As you make exercise a daily part of your life, you will be provided with significant stress relief, energy, and optimism.

To incorporate more exercise into your busy life, use the following tips:

☐ **Check with your doctor to ensure you are healthy enough for exercise.** For example, if you have bad knees or chronic back pain, your doctor might advise you to avoid activities that will exacerbate the strain on your joints, like running, and instead advise you toward activities that better fit your body's specific needs. If you

---

[7] Birte von Haaren, Joerg Ottenbacher, Julia Muenz, Rainer Neumann, Klaus Boes, and Ulrich Ebner-Priemer, "Does a 20-Week Aerobic Exercise Training Programme Increase Our Capabilities to Buffer Real-Life Stressors? A Randomized, Controlled Trial Using Ambulatory Assessment," *European Journal of Applied Physiology* 116, no. 2 (February 2016): 383–394, https://doi.org/10.1007/s00421-015-3284-8.

CHAPTER 5: Embrace the Benefits of Stress Management

have a physical disability, you may be able to play adaptive sports to get the exercise you need.

☐ **Build up your exercise routine gradually.** No one begins his or her exercise routine running marathons, so be patient with yourself in your first few weeks. For example, if you have never run before, consider walking a few miles before you increase your pace to jogging, then running.

☐ **Perform exercise that you enjoy.** If you hate running, do not run. If you do, you will be more likely to stop your exercise routine before you achieve worthwhile results. Consider joining group workout classes after work or lifting weights with a friend a few times each week. If you make exercise a fun and social activity, you will be more inclined to integrate it as an everyday part of your life.

☐ **Schedule regular workout sessions like you would a meeting.** By treating your workouts seriously, you will be less likely to cancel. Consider working out in the morning if possible, as studies have shown that people are more likely to stick to a morning workout routine than an evening one.[8] You are more likely to skip an evening workout due to weariness, hunger, or having already scheduled other activities earlier in the day.

Improve Your Sleep Patterns

Many people experience significant reactions to otherwise minimal stressors due to a lack of sleep. Consider the last time you snapped at someone due to exhaustion or had an exaggerated reaction to a relatively small issue. You might have reacted differently if you had an optimal amount of sleep

---

[8] Kaitlyn Bailey and Mary Jung, "The Early Bird Gets the Worm! Congruency Between Intentions and Behavior is Highest When Plans to Exercise are Made for the Morning," *Journal Of Applied Biobehavioral Research* 19, no. 4 (December 2014): 233–247, https://doi.org/10.1111/jabr.12027.

the previous night. Your sleep schedule is a critical factor of any effective stress management regime. If you constantly deprive yourself of proper sleep, or if you habitually oversleep, you will be more likely to experience depression, anxiety, mood swings, and other negative emotions that are commonly associated with stress. By allowing yourself the optimal amount of sleep, you will be able to handle certain stressors in a more calm and relaxed manner. Refer to and incorporate the sleep techniques listed in Chapter 4 to experience better sleep quality and reduced stress.

Understand Your Stressors

If you want to fight back against stress in the workplace, it helps to understand when you start feeling the most stressed. Stress rarely manifests at a consistent level; instead, it occurs in peaks and waves depending on the stressors you are exposed to. By remembering certain reactions and the situations that stimulated them, you will understand which stressors must be minimized as frequently as possible. To become more aware of your stressors and the activities you can use to cope with them, use the following steps:

1. **Keep a journal of your emotions throughout the week.** Ensure your records are as detailed as possible, especially when you start feeling anxious, stressed, or angry. After writing down your emotional state, try to identify the stressor: what were you thinking about, or what happened to make you feel that way? Even if you are not certain of the cause, write down your assumptions. This reflection will help you more easily identify the scenarios and situations that cause you to react in a stressed manner.

Emotion:	Stressor:
Anxious	Traffic was bad during commute
Stressed	Manager moved deadline sooner
Angry	Coworker misplaced my documents

2. **When you have identified which stressors make you feel anxious or depressed, record various techniques you can use to minimize them.** For example, if you often feel stressed during your morning commute, consider taking different routes, or investing in a relaxing music album you can listen to while you commute. If a certain manager in your workplace causes you to feel anxious, consider submitting a request to your supervisor to work under someone else.

3. **Record the activities and people who produce positive sensations.** For example, if you always feel happy talking with your grandmother, consider calling her after work to relieve feelings of stress. Also consider investing in a gym membership, which is a proven method for reducing feelings of stress and anxiety.[9]

> Positivity List:
> Talk with grandma
> Play basketball with friends
> Read an exciting book
> Listen to music
> Go for a jog
> Meditate

Reframe Your Perception of Stress

An IRS audit, losing important documents, or a major argument with your manager are all undeniably stressful experiences, even to an individual with a high tolerance for stress. However, one supposition of constructive thinking is

---

[9] Birte von Haaren, Joerg Ottenbacher, Julia Muenz, Rainer Neumann, Klaus Boes, and Ulrich Ebner-Priemer, "Does a 20-Week Aerobic Exercise Training Programme Increase Our Capabilities to Buffer Real-Life Stressors? A Randomized, Controlled Trial Using Ambulatory Assessment," *European Journal of Applied Physiology* 116, no. 2 (February 2016): 383–394, https://doi.org/10.1007/s00421-015-3284-8.

CHAPTER 5: Embrace the Benefits of Stress Management

that the stimuli itself is not stressful, but rather the individual's *perception* of the stimuli is stressful.

Cognitive reframing is a method for intentionally viewing events in ways that create less stress and promote more feelings of positivity, peace, and control.[10] Reframing techniques are based on the principle that your body's stress response is triggered by *perceived* stress, not actual events. For example, suppose you accidentally delete a report from your computer, and so you will now be late for your deadline. Suddenly, your thoughts spiral out of control. You think about the eventual scolding you will receive from your boss or your client. You may even believe the mistake will result in you being fired from your company. Before you know it, you are in full-blown "panic mode" as you wonder how you will be able to pay your bills and rent, or even find another job.

There is no need to let your thoughts spiral to this stressful state. In order to change your perception of stressful events, use the following strategies whenever you start feeling signs of stress and anxiety:

☐ **Recount the stressful situation as if it were an event in a story.** Rather than immediately jumping to the conclusion that you are not a good fit for your career (which is stressful thinking), weave the scenario into a story, and refer to your role in the third-person. For example, you might think to yourself, "John has only managed this project for two weeks. When John came onto the project, it was four weeks behind. While the project may still be late, John has moved the project to being only one week behind, not four." This storytelling tactic helps you understand that your failures are often sprinkled with successes. Also, by stepping away from the stressful incident, you escape from your negative thoughts

---

[10] Elizabeth Scott, "4 Steps to Shift Perspective and Change Everything: How to Reframe Situations so They Create Less Stress," Verywell Mind, last modified November 26, 2018, https://www.verywellmind.com/cognitive-reframing-for-stress-management-3144872.

CHAPTER 5: Embrace the Benefits of Stress Management

and identify valuable lessons that might be applied in your future.

☐ **Give yourself a reality check or ask a friend to provide one.** Being reprimanded by a manager might convince you that you are a poor fit for your job or that you will soon be fired. However, challenging these stressful thoughts with reality checks allows you to stop them before you resort to contemplating life as a homeless person. Reality checks have a profound positive impact on your mental health and well-being because they prevent your stressful thoughts from increasing. Observe the following two examples of how reality checks can address a stressful situations:

✗ **Stressful Thought:** "I was laid off because I am a failure as a person, and I will never be hired again."

✓ **Realistic Thought:** "I was laid off due to company restructuring, and I will quickly update my resume and start searching for jobs."

✗ **Stressful Thought:** "My manager was curt to me this morning. He will certainly fire me."

✓ **Realistic Thought:** "My manager was curt to me this morning. He may have had a bad time in traffic or a troublesome incident at home."

☐ **Remind yourself of times when you were successful.** In our busy lives, we often forget times when we achieved success in past situations. Despite having evidence of our abilities to accomplish wonderful things, we still foresee the worst possible outcome. This is often referred to as "exaggerated negative thinking."

If exaggerated negative thinking is persistent in your thought process, write a list of goals you have accomplished. Ideally, they should relate to your professional career; however, major personal triumphs, like losing weight or training for a marathon, can provide the boost you need to believe in yourself. By countering your negative thoughts with challenging evidence, you will ingrain positive thoughts into your subconscious, thus reducing the amount of stress you experience when interpreting present life scenarios.

Restructure Your Life

Restructuring your life involves using systems or models to streamline your everyday life. This process increases your capability for handling stressful events when they occur. Consider using the following strategies to open yourself up to the stress-releasing benefits of life structuring:

- [ ] **Accept personal responsibility.** We often assign negative connotations to the idea of responsibility. However, when you rethink this key term, you will realize that accepting responsibility for your past mistakes provides you with an immediate sense of empowerment. For example, if you have ever found yourself frantically working late to meet a deadline, reconsider your behaviors that might have put you in that position. You might discover that your own actions, such as procrastinating on the task or failing to plan your work, led to this stressful position. By examining the personal behaviors which placed you in your past stressful situations, you can devise strategies for avoiding similar scenarios in the future.

☐ **Allow yourself time for inner reflection.** This is a semi-meditative technique that allows you to identify all the positives you have in your life, while establishing a healthy sense of perspective when you are caught up in a stressful situation. For example, if you have been working on a major project throughout your entire shift, it might be tempting to bring this stress home with you. However, give yourself time for positive inner reflection. You probably have food in your stomach and a roof over your head. You might have a beautiful family who loves you dearly, or friends who enjoy hearing from you. When we appreciate what we have in life, we rise above stressful situations at work.

While the above stress management techniques will prove useful in a variety of workplace scenarios and personal strife, the mental disarray caused by some stress-inducing life events might be too severe for such methods to work as intended. In these cases, alternative measures must be taken.

Seek Professional Help as Necessary

People often overcome workplace setbacks when given time and clarity. However, certain life events are so inherently stressful that they necessitate the guidance of a professional counselor or therapist. In 1967, Thomas Holmes and Richard Rahe sought to research the major life changes that manifested the greatest stress levels within individuals. Their results make up what is now known as the Social Readjustment Rating Scale (SRRS), a tool that is used by health and social science disciplines.[11] The SRRS finds that the following major life changes are the most significant stressors (ranked from least to most stressful):

---

[11] Saul McLeod, "Stress and Life Events," Simply Psychology, accessed November 1, 2018, https://www.simplypsychology.org/SRRS.html.

CHAPTER 5: Embrace the Benefits of Stress Management

Life Change:	Stress Value:
Retirement	45
Marital Reconciliation	45
Fired at work	47
Marriage	50
Personal injury or illness	53
Death of a close family member	63
Incarceration	63
Marital separation	65
Divorce	73
Death of a spouse	100

Many stress researchers argue that, due to our nature as gregarious creatures, our social environment has a fundamental impact on our abilities to cope with certain scenarios. You might recognize that the most stressful life events presented in the SRRS typically force us to adapt to new social environments.

If you think you may benefit from professional help with your stress or anxiety, do not berate yourself. These professionals are trained in helping individuals address stressful life in a healthy manner. Use the following assessment to determine whether you might benefit from professional help:

☐ You have tried to deal with your stress using stress management techniques, but it continues to manifest in unhealthy ways.

☐ You have suffered several major setbacks, and you feel like you need help bouncing back.

☐ Your stress is affecting your quality of life, and you feel like you are spiralling into anxiety and depression.

☐ You have developed several medical problems due to your high-stress lifestyle, or you always feel sick.

☐ You need help developing your coping skills, as you are unable to put stress management techniques to use.

Ultimately, talking to a professional counselor or therapist about your stressful lifestyle is one of the wisest steps you can take toward restoring the quality of your life. Refusing to seek help might severely impact your ability to uphold a healthy and balanced life. You probably will not hesitate to meet with your doctor about physical injury or illness, so meet with your counselor or therapist to care for your mental health in the same way. Do not wait for stress to manifest itself in physical illness. Instead, seek the help of a counselor or therapist to learn new strategies for handling stress in your life.

Conclusion

As you have now learned, becoming an indispensable employee means focusing on your vision of success, defining achievable action steps, adjusting to your workplace, making rational and dependable decisions, and staying cool and confident in the face of stressful workplace scenarios. When your supervisors notice you demonstrating these instrumental skills, they will entrust you with greater responsibility and appraise your value in the workplace.

Becoming an indispensable member of your workplace is not necessarily about having the most unique talents or the most impressive degrees. It is not even about your position in your department. When employers envision a valuable employee, they often see someone who is dependable, reliable, and who can always be counted on to present high-quality work when it is needed the most. Let us return to the example of Joe, who successfully implements the proficiency skills detailed in this book to establish himself as an indispensable member of his workplace:

***

Example: Joe

Joe is an administrative assistant at a mid-sized vintage and indie clothing company. During a period of aggressive company growth, Joe becomes a particularly vital component of the workplace. Joe does not highlight his value with industry-specific knowledge, but rather he establishes himself as a trustworthy employee capable of enduring the most troubling workplace dilemmas. Consider the following situations in which Joe proves himself to be a valued asset:

CONCLUSION

- **Joe commits to conscious improvement of professional character traits, such as integrity, persistence, and self-discipline.** He implements an unwavering focus on achieving his dreams: having more responsibility for growing his company and attaining a greater sense of peace in his professional and personal lives. This focus naturally encourages him to consistently output high-quality work.

- **Joe creates clear, measurable, and time-sensitive goals.** He steadily makes progress toward his goal of obtaining more leadership positions by taking realistic action steps, such as asking his supervisor to lead team meetings. He also regularly checks his progress by asking for feedback and performing quarterly self-assessments of his achievements.

- **Joe adapts to match the demands and culture of his workplace.** By demonstrating standard workplace manners, learning from more seasoned coworkers, and using technology appropriately, Joe develops positive relationships with his fellow professionals.

- **Joe confidently makes independent decisions and implements them in his workplace.** Joe finds this ability especially useful during the transitional time in his workplace, as his supervisors are often occupied by other tasks or activities, and Joe does not always have time to seek approval for each of his decisions. Joe persists by researching his options, carefully assessing his alternatives, detailing the necessary steps for any action, and confidently implementing his decisions when it is time to do so.

- **Joe embraces the benefits of stress management, which enables him to stay cool and collected even throughout the most intense seasons.** By organizing his workspace, maintaining his physical health, and mindfully tempering of his reactivity to stressful stimuli,

CONCLUSION

Joe accomplishes all his projects despite quick deadlines. He is looked upon by his coworkers as an inspiration.

Thanks to Joe's hard work, passion, and diligent attitude, he gains the trust and support of his organization. Joe requests to be reassigned to a greater job role where he can continue to use his proficiency skills to benefit his company, find a sense of purpose, and earn the satisfaction of many jobs well done. His managers wholeheartedly approve this decision.

***

Joe did not have a plethora of degrees, nor an inherent talent that made him stand out in the workplace. Instead, he recognized that one of the best pathways to achieving his goal and earning a new title as an office manager was to become an incredibly valuable and versatile member of his workplace. As the example demonstrates, success in the workplace does not depend on an innate personality trait. By developing the learnable skills described in this book you can achieve professional success much like Joe did.

If you are still not sure how to identify a proficient employee, simply find the person that a manager or supervisor can point to and say, "I can count on that individual to do the right thing." This dependability is the heart of achieving your loftiest professional goal, be it supporting your community or just becoming a more valued member of your department. When others count on you, you stand out as a person that should be provided with more leadership opportunities.

Remember, the valuable skills taught in this book are not ingrained in only a few specific people. They are readily available to anyone who is willing to pursue them. You do not have to possess a superhuman talent or prestigious degree to become a proficient employee. You simply need to focus on learning and continually improving the skills taught in this book: envisioning success, setting achievable goals, adjusting to your workplace, making decisions, and managing stress.

CONCLUSION

Integrating these skills into your life may be challenging, but this is an achievable journey. So long as you are willing to persevere through adversity and steadily hone your abilities, the skills explained in this book will take you to any summit you can imagine.

About the Author

Phillip Selleh has led organizations on both a national and an international scale by providing management to companies including AT&T, Inc., a world leader in communications, media, entertainment, and technology; META Group, a leading information technology research and consulting firm; Computer Sciences Corporation, a provider of information technology and professional services; and Ontempo eServices, a provider of business intelligence and marketing solutions. While hospitalized at Walter Reed National Military Medical Center during military service, Phillip Selleh interacted with service members who expressed interest in transitioning to careers in business and overcoming the obstacles to achieving their goals. These interactions inspired him to found and become a board member of About Giving, Inc. A 501(c)(3) Public Charity, About Giving, Inc., provides educational opportunities and high-quality resources to severely disabled Veterans in need of assistance. Phillip Selleh earned a Master of Business Administration in Entrepreneural and International Finance from George Washington University. He also gained education and training in leadership and operations from the United States Army before retiring as a Colonel.

Phillip Selleh now dedicates his unique skills and abilities toward aiding other severely disabled Veterans with professional career development at the Center for Business Acceleration (CenterForBusinessAcceleration.com/Veteran).

www.ingramcontent.com/pod-product-compliance
Lightning Source LLC
Chambersburg PA
CBHW050204170426
42811CB00130B/2201/J